A HORRIBLE END, OR AN END TO THE HORROR?

by Bob Avakian

RCP Publications
Chicago

Library of Congress Cataloging in Publication Data

Avakian, Bob.
A horrible end, or, An end to the horror?

1. Revolutions and socialism—United States.
2. Nuclear warfare. 3. Disarmament. 4. Peace.
I. Title. II. Title: Horrible end. III. Title:
End to the horror?
HX550.R48A93 1984 320.5′31 84-18215
ISBN 0-89851-070-8 (pbk.)

First Printing: 1984
Second Printing: 1986
Printed in U.S.A.

Published by:
RCP Publications
P.O. Box 3486 Merchandise Mart
Chicago, IL U.S.A. 60654

Bob Avakian is Chairman of the Revolutionary Communist Party, USA. A major voice on the revolutionary left since the 1960s, he was active in the Free Speech and antiwar movements in Berkeley, worked closely with the Black Panther Party, figured prominently in debates within the Students for a Democratic Society, and founded the Revolutionary Union in 1968. Avakian quickly emerged as the leading Maoist thinker in the United States, and has over the last fifteen years written numerous analyses of the world situation and problems of revolutionary strategy. His previously published works include *The Loss in China and the Revolutionary Legacy of Mao Tsetung*, *Mao Tsetung's Immortal Contributions*, *Conquer the World? The International Proletariat Must and Will*, and *For a Harvest of Dragons*. In 1980, under threat of more than a lifetime in jail — as a result of trumped-up charges stemming from a demonstration against Deng Xiaoping in 1979 — Bob Avakian was forced into exile in France.

CONTENTS

INTRODUCTION: WAR AND REVOLUTION

The question of world war — the growing, imminent danger of war between two equally imperialist blocs, one headed by the USA and the other headed by the USSR — is the most acute problem in the world today. This is not some kind of "accidental" phenomenon, nor is it the expression of the subjective attitudes or actions of individuals, no matter how powerful. It is rather the expression of profound objective contradictions which have reached a decisive conjuncture: it represents a concentration of the "normal workings" of the imperialist system and at the same time a tremendous magnification of them and their destructive consequences for the great majority of the world's people, for humanity as a whole. This poses new and genuinely unprecedented problems, even as compared to previous explosions of the world contradictions of imperialism with previous world wars.

The present world-historic conjuncture shaping up, the intense gathering together and heightening of the major contradictions in the world in this period, is in an overall way magnified many times beyond — in fact it is qualitatively beyond — previous conjunctures of this kind focused around the two previous world wars. Thus not only the dangers and potentially destructive consequences but also the possibilities for revolutionary breakthroughs, for the overthrow of reactionary social systems and for profound revolutionary changes in the entire structure of world relations, are greatly heightened.

The relation (or dialectic) between war and revolution is at the center of this historic drama being enacted in the world arena: a deadly serious struggle is going on between these two trends which will have everything to do with determining the direction of human society, and indeed the destiny of humanity itself. The question of revolution is very much alive — and more, it represents the only possible way forward. This, again, is all the more so because the whole world and its future are this time, quite literally, at stake. Any other attempted solution to this, which will leave the foundations of imperialism untouched and bring no fundamental changes in world relations and social systems, is utterly incapable of providing a way forward out of this howling madness; *only* proletarian revolution holds the possibility for doing so.

The formation of the Revolutionary Internationalist Movement is a tremendous advance out of the setback and disarray experienced by the international communist movement in the wake of the loss in China (following only two decades after the restoration of capitalism in the Soviet Union). The formation of the Revolutionary Internationalist Movement represents a very significant regrouping of the international forces of proletarian revolution and a real change in the equation of world relations — it represents a leap in the potential to confront and transform the world situation, including the possibility of actually preventing world war through revolution. As the *Declaration of the Revolutionary Internationalist Movement* states, "only the advance of the world revolution can stop the war in preparation and attack its source."[1] And as I formulated it recently, "only the seizure of

[1] *Declaration of the Revolutionary Internationalist Movement* (English edition, 1984), p. 43. This *Declaration* was issued on May 1, 1984 in 22 languages and is being distributed in all parts of the world. It was adopted by the delegates and observers of the Second International Conference of Marxist-Leninist Parties and Organisations which formed the Revolutionary Internationalist Movement:

Central Reorganisation Committee, Communist Party of India (Marxist-Leninist)
Ceylon Communist Party
Communist Collective of Agit/Prop [Italy]
Communist Party of Colombia (Marxist-Leninist) Mao Tsetung Regional Committee
Communist Party of Peru
Communist Party of Turkey/Marxist-Leninist
Haitian International Revolutionary Group
Nepal Communist Party (Mashal)

power by the proletariat in large and/or strategic enough parts of the world to qualitatively alter the whole equation of world relations — can prevent world war, and on the other hand if world war does break out, with all its terrible destruction, that will in fact heighten the possibilities for revolution, which remains the only way forward out of all this madness and destruction."[2]

Perhaps, if things are looked at narrowly, and specifically are seen from only a U.S. or European (or "developed country") perspective, this statement — and particularly the second part about the possibilities for revolution being heightened if war does break out — may seem unrealistic, even wildly out of touch with reality; but if things are truly viewed from a worldwide and world-historic perspective, this orientation is of even greater importance than ever before, *precisely because* of what the stakes are this time. With this kind of orientation and understanding it is possible to grasp more deeply the profound correctness and significance of the statement by Mao Tsetung cited in the *Declaration of the Revolutionary Internationalist Movement*: "Either revolution will prevent [world] war, or [world] war will give rise to revolution."[3] Given the stakes that have been spoken of — and in particular the actual consequences of a world war that would almost certainly involve major nuclear exchanges — it is not only correct but crucial to give great emphasis to the question of preventing this war. But at the same time we must struggle all the more to win people to the understanding that only the advance of the world proletarian revolution holds the

---

New Zealand Red Flag Group
Nottingham and Stockport Communist Groups [Britain]
Proletarian Communist Organization, Marxist-Leninist [Italy]
Proletarian Party of Purba Bangla [Bangladesh]
Revolutionary Communist Group of Colombia
Revolutionary Communist Party, India
Revolutionary Communist Party, USA
Revolutionary Communist Union [Dominican Republic]
Union of Iranian Communists (Sarbedaran)

[2] "World War Must Be Opposed With Revolution, Not Peace," *Revolutionary Worker* (*RW*), No. 227 (October 21, 1983), p. 3.

[3] Cited in the *Declaration of the Revolutionary Internationalist Movement*, p. 7.

possibility for doing this, and the tendency to think that literally nothing will be possible — at least nothing positive — if such a war breaks out must be vigorously and sharply refuted. In all this, the Revolutionary Internationalist Movement has a tremendously important role to play, and every effort must be extended to support, strengthen, and develop it to realize its full potential to profoundly affect world events in the period before us, which will represent a turning point without precedent in human society.

At the same time, special responsibilities as well as particular opportunities to affect world events exist in the U.S., given the kind of country it is and the role it plays in world relations. It was recently reported to me that a comrade from another country who has been deeply involved in intense struggles between revolution and counterrevolution there posed in a very frank and earnest way the question: when are you (our party in the U.S.) going to launch the revolutionary struggle for power? This was asked not as a criticism or with unthinking impatience, but with the open — and very correct — urging that such a struggle, launched when and as soon as the conditions emerged for doing so and launched with a perspective for fighting through to win, would be a powerful blow for the world revolution and a great assistance and encouragement to the revolutionary proletariat in its struggle everywhere. It is in unity with this spirit and orientation that this book is being written and that it will focus to a large extent on a number of major questions related to the revolutionary struggle in the U.S. — touching especially on the actual possibility for revolution in such a country and the strategy for actually carrying out the revolutionary struggle to overthrow U.S. imperialism and establish proletarian rule. But this will also be taken up in the context of world relations and struggles and the world-historic problem of communist revolution in a global environment still ruled, distorted, and threatened with massive destruction by imperialism.

Hence the title of this book: *A Horrible End, or An End to the Horror?* A horrible end — at least to human civilization as it has developed to this point — that is a very real possibility posed in the period ahead; it is to this threshold that the development of civilization under the domination of exploiting classes and their oppressive states has brought us. And such a horrible end is something to be actively, urgently fought against. But at the same time, it must never be forgotten that the daily workings of this system are a continual horror for the great majority of the world's people — this is no exaggeration but a profound, searing truth commonly overlooked in the preserves of privilege and comfort that exist for broad strata much of the time in the imperialist citadels. Nor must it be forgotten that, as stressed earlier, the only possible means of preventing such a horrible end, or in any case the only way forward in the face of it, is the advance of the world proletarian revolution.

To quote again the *Declaration of the Revolutionary Internationalist Movement* on this crucial point:

> Communists are resolute opponents of imperialist war and must mobilise and lead the masses in the fight against preparations for a third world war which would be the greatest crime committed in the history of mankind. But the Marxist-Leninists will never hide the truth from the masses: only revolution, revolutionary war that the Marxist-Leninists and revolutionary forces are leading or preparing to lead, can prevent this crime. . . . If, on the other hand, the revolutionary struggle is not capable of preventing a third world war, the communists and the revolutionary proletariat and masses must be prepared to mobilise the outrage that such a war and the inevitable suffering accompanying it will engender and direct it against the source of war — imperialism, take advantage of the weakened position of the enemy and in this way turn a reactionary imperialist war into a just war against imperialism and reaction.[4]

Thus the question is not whether there will be sacrifice, even heightened suffering for a period, but of what kind, yes of what magnitude but most fundamentally toward what end: A Horrible End, or An End to the Horror?

The stakes involved and the urgency of these questions de-

[4] *Declaration of the Revolutionary Internationalist Movement*, pp. 7-8.

mand that they be taken up in a penetrating and thoroughgoing way and unshrinkingly grappled with not only by the advanced, politically conscious forces, on the international level as well as within the different countries, but also by broader masses as they are awakened to political life. It is more crucial than ever that these questions and their profound implications be made accessible to all those who are concerned and must be concerned with these questions and are, potentially at least, part of the solution and not part of the problem.

With the above as an introduction, I'll turn now to the main substance of this book.

I.

The Challenge:

More on the Urgent Necessity and the Actual Strategy for Making Revolution in a Country Like the U.S. — More on Charting the Uncharted Course

NUCLEAR WAR — POLITICAL AND IDEOLOGICAL QUESTIONS

The Godfather

Here I'm referring specifically to the end of the movie *Godfather I*. After Vito Corleone has died and Sonny, the impetuous and volatile son who held sway for a brief and stormy interregnum, has been gunned down, Michael, the "pure bourgeois" godfather, takes over. In the closing scenes — which are very powerfully done — Michael is acting, literally, as the godfather for his sister's newborn child, solemnly swearing to renounce Satan and his deeds, while one by one we see his opponents being gunned down in cold blood (from the Las Vegas hotel-casino owner to all of Michael's rivals in New York and New Jersey, etc.). Through back and forth between the baptism and the murders we see Michael repeating, "I do renounce them," not only with a straight face but in a very sanctimonious way while at the very same time his orders are being carried out to gun people down — deeds worthy of the devil's deeds he's denouncing.

Then at the end of all that there's a final scene where his sister comes in and accuses him, rightly, of having murdered her husband — on top of these other assassinations — because he betrayed the family. But when she accuses him of this he basically passes it off as "feminine hysteria" and tries to "calm her down." And then she goes out, having rebuked him — "you're so heartless, you murdered the father of the very child you just acted as godfather for." Michael's wife is there and has witnessed this scene; she looks up at him searchingly and says, "Michael, is it true?" He slams down his fist and says, "Never ask me about my affairs! Never ask me about my business!" But she persists and finally he says, "Okay, this one time. This one time you can ask me." So she looks at him as if to repeat the question "is it true?" And he says, "No, it's not true." With an absolutely straight face!

I think there's a lesson here. There are many lessons here on many different levels, but to make a summary: here we have Michael Corleone having coldly executed a series of synchronized murders while he wears the straight face of respectability and swears pious sanctity, even acting as godfather for a child whose father's murder he has already ordered. What can we learn from this? This is a glimpse into the inner nature of the imperialists — both superpowers and both blocs of imperialists. If we take for example the 007 airplane incident and look at the rationales on both sides it is straight gangster logic all the way around. Imperialist provocation and response on the basis of straight gangster logic: "We are world powers in a confrontation for who will dominate the world and on that basis nobody's gonna fuck with us." That, I think, is something that holds some very important lessons for us.

What is the rationale and what is the whole posture taken by the one side and the other? On the one hand in creating the provocation — which was clearly engineered by the U.S. — and on the other hand in not only responding in the expected way but then in the rationale that was given and the posture that was struck by the Soviet Union, it is imperialist maneuvering, positioning and contending, and gangster logic all the way around. Or you can take the missile deployments in Europe and the arguments and maneuvering around them on both sides, which we've been treated to in the last year or so. Or El Salvador and Nicaragua on the one hand and Afghanistan and Poland on the other. In all these cases and in innumerable other cases that could be cited, the straight-up imperialist gangster logic used as justification by the imperialists on both sides is very striking. And as I said, the examples could be multiplied many times over.

Both sides are imperialist. Both are driven by the same inner compulsion of the laws (or contradictions) of the imperialist system and the world conjuncture to which this is leading. Both of them are Michael Corleones. Both will swear and are swearing with pious sanctity and an absolutely straight face that they do not intend to do and would never think of doing — that in fact they renounce — the very thing for which they are preparing: world war with all of its destruction. Yes, they *will* do it — go to war with each other and engage in major nuclear exchanges in an effort to win that war. They *will* do it — if they aren't stopped — and every effort must be exerted to stop them! And intense ideological struggle and debate must be waged over the momentous question: what is necessary to actually stop them?

Here it is necessary to refute the rather widely propagated notion, including within the "peace movement" (in its broadest definition), that such a war and such nuclear exchanges will not happen because neither side could win, and if nothing else they are both capable enough of recognizing their own interests and therefore of refraining from such a mutually destructive and self-defeating enterprise. Or, as a companion argument to this, it is said that if such a war did break out it would be due to an "accident" or "misjudgment" of some kind, a danger which is said to be great now because of the spiraling arms race and the current very intense atmosphere of confrontation and belligerency on both sides.

Thus, according to this argument, the essential step to bring these superpowers, and mankind, back from the brink of Armageddon is to reverse the arms race and take real steps toward eventual disarmament and to cool out the tension and "hot spots" in the international geopolitical scene. This is not infrequently coupled with the insistence that, whatever one thinks of the Soviet Union, it is not imperialist like the U.S., it is not driven to war by the same inner compulsion of the imperialist system, and its huge military apparatus and arms budget, its involvement in the "arms race" and even its military adventures and interventions are of an essentially defensive nature, in reaction to the aggressiveness and bellicosity of the U.S., or at least certain

U.S. administrations (such as the Reagan Administration). But, in one form or another — and whether apologetic for the Soviet Union or not — this kind of argument is forced to deny the fundamental truth that it is the contradictions and motion of imperialism and its fundamental and essential nature that is right now propelling things toward the brink of world war and nuclear devastation.

For example, one of the leading spokesmen for this view, one of the prominent figures in the established "peace movement" in England (and Europe), E.P. Thompson, has insisted that "the present war crisis" is "being willed by no single causative historical logic ('the increasingly aggressive military posture of world imperialism,' etc.) — a logic which then may be analysed in terms of origins, intentions or goals, contradictions or conjunctures" but is "simply the product of a messy inertia"[5] — the continuing momentum and influence of the Cold War, the arms race, the military-industrial complex, and so forth. Thompson further argues that not only world war itself but even the massive military expenditures on both sides at the present time are irrational — from their own point of view. Therefore, world war and nuclear devastation are avoidable, if the people act as a massive popular force, a counterweight to this inertia — and if they do so act they can not only prevent this inertia from dragging the world into nuclear Armageddon but can also eventually bring about a radical change in the present military blocs and whole new possibilities for peaceful realignments and other major political changes in the world (peaceful at least in the sense that the threat of world war/nuclear devastation will have been removed).[6]

Sometimes arguments such as these are presented as a "refutation" of the basic principle formulated by the nineteenth-century German military writer and scholar Carl von Clausewitz, a principle upheld and propagated by Lenin (and later by Mao), that war is the continuation of politics by other, military, means.

[5] E.P. Thompson, *Beyond the Cold War* (New York: Pantheon Books, 1982), p. 41.

[6] Thompson, *Beyond the Cold War*, p. 76.

This "refutation" insists that since neither side can win such a world war involving major nuclear exchanges, then this war, if it occurred, could not be the expression or extension of conscious policy aims of either side, but could only result from accidental causes (as referred to above) or at most could express the interests of military cliques or a military-industrial complex within the elites of both sides, as opposed to the general self-interest of the ruling classes as a whole. Or such an argument might be presented as an *application* of the Clausewitzian principle, but "in reverse": that is, since such a war could only be self-defeating for both sides and bring mutual destruction (as well as the annihilation of human civilization, at least as we have known it), then the extension of the political objectives on both sides — to ensure dominance and the ability to exploit — would lead not to the waging but to the avoiding of war with the other side, armed as it is with the same weapons of mutual destruction.

The problem with this line of reasoning is that it ignores the fundamental fact that the very logic — the inner contradiction and motion — of imperialism has now brought things to the point where both sides desperately need a qualitative change in the whole structure of world relations *and each stands as the direct barrier to the other in achieving this.* Or, as I wrote in the article, "World War Must Be Opposed With Revolution, Not Peace," for the imperialists — and not just the ruling classes of the superpowers but all the imperialists — on both sides "the world cannot much longer go on as it is anyway — it must be forcibly recast in order for that system to lurch ahead for a time once again and for their positions to be strengthened and secured at the expense of their rivals and of the masses of people in the world."[7]

It is for this reason that even massive outpourings of pro-

[7] "World War Must Be Opposed With Revolution," *RW*, No. 227, p. 3. Here, as in this article, I urge people — especially those who would dismiss this as dogma or rhetoric — to seriously study and grapple with the profound analysis of this found in Raymond Lotta with Frank Shannon, *America in Decline: An Analysis of the Developments Toward War and Revolution, in the U.S. and Worldwide, in the 1980s*, Vol. 1 (Chicago: Banner Press, 1984).

test in Europe and elsewhere have failed to halt the deployment of the cruise and Pershing missiles in Europe.[8] Take, for example, the insistence of the Western imperialists to go ahead with this deployment in the face of acknowledged majority opposition in West Germany and massive protest in many other countries (and let us keep in mind that the original decision to deploy was made while a Democrat, Carter, was President in the U.S. and Social Democrats headed the government in West Germany). How can this — or for that matter the corresponding moves and countermeasures by the Soviet bloc — be considered the outcome of "inertia" or simply the product of a so-called military-industrial complex, on one or both sides, somehow standing above, even in opposition to, the ruling classes as a whole and their rational self-interest? It is now more than ever a dangerous delusion, or self-delusion, to propagate such theories which fail or refuse to reckon with and deal with reality as it is and as it is developing, ever more rapidly, toward an apocalyptic eruption.

In fact, the present accelerating motion toward war, on both sides, is a dramatic illustration of the principle enunciated by Clausewitz, a principle which has not infrequently been vulgarized, especially by those who deny its validity. Clausewitz argued that while war is something qualitatively different from politics per se, war never exists in pure form, exactly because it is "nothing but a continuation of political intercourse, with a mixture of other means." Clausewitz continues: "We say mixed with other means in order thereby to maintain at the same time that this political intercourse does not cease by the War itself, is not

[8] The case of the Netherlands, where the government has delayed deployment, in part at least because of domestic political considerations, does not alter the fundamental point here. It does not outweigh the overwhelming fact that the key missiles are being installed, and even if we were to assume that the government of the Netherlands would actually refuse once and for all to have these missiles deployed — which it has *not* done and which it is not likely to do — the existence of this one "exception" not only is the "exception that proves the rule" but no doubt would be turned to political advantage by the "Western democratic" bloc of imperialists — cited as proof of "the right of dissent" setting it apart from the rival Soviet bloc and providing yet another illustration of why it is well worth fighting and dying for!

changed into something quite different, but that, in its essence, it continues to exist, whatever may be the form of the means which it uses, and that the chief lines on which the events of the War progress, and to which they are attached, are only the general features of policy which run all through the War until peace takes place."[9] In other words, war is throughout commanded, guided, by the political objectives for which it is being fought; and the means used in the war, including the deployment of different weapons, their actual use, etc., are influenced and overall determined by these political objectives — even though war does "have a life of its own."

It is consistent with — and not a refutation of — this basic principle that the military strategists and planners, as well as the overall political leaders, on both sides are attempting to find the means for fighting *and winning* a war, one that will involve large-scale nuclear exchanges, with the other bloc. The fact that it is very, very unlikely that all their planning and strategic thinking can accomplish the objective of fighting and winning such a war without in the process bringing about the destruction of much of human civilization as it exists today — this too is not a refutation of the "Clausewitzian principle": such a war would still be an attempt (again by both sides) to achieve political objectives (serving underlying economic interests) by military means, and it would not be the first time in history that such an attempt led to failure and destruction on both sides, though it would certainly be the most profound and cataclysmic instance.

The recent criticisms, proposals, etc., from such people as Robert McNamara (Defense Secretary under Kennedy and Johnson, during the Vietnam War) and Democratic presidential candidate Gary Hart, are precisely attempts to deal with this contradiction and to come up with a military strategy and nuclear policy capable of waging and surviving — surviving as the *victor* — a war involving significant nuclear exchanges with

[9] Carl von Clausewitz, *On War*, edited with an introduction by Anatol Rapoport (Middlesex, England: Penguin Books, 1983), p. 402.

the Soviet bloc. As analyzed in our party's newspaper, the *Revolutionary Worker*, in general terms such strategic thinking — and the thrust of the criticism of current policy and doctrine — emphasizes more flexibility in place of overwhelming reliance on massive nuclear strikes or the threat of them — but *not* in place of the *use* of nukes. Beefed-up conventional forces; rapid strikes deep into Soviet-bloc territory to "intermingle" with Warsaw Pact troops and thereby to some degree "neutralize" nuclear attacks on NATO troops in this situation; the possibility of holding off from using "the nuclear option" for awhile — while reaping full propaganda value from pulling back from the up-to-now *declared* (and never renounced) first-strike policy of the U.S. — and at all costs ensuring the "survivability" of the U.S. (and NATO) nuclear arsenals for "retaliation"; more emphasis on mobility and "fast-tempo attacks" and the kind of changes in doctrine and weapons production that would necessarily go along with this: these are some examples of the attempts of such "critics" to contribute to the cause of propagandizing peace and of actually winning the war "in some recognizable sense," as the *Revolutionary Worker* so incisively put it.[10]

It is crucial to point out here and to continually expose the fact that nuclear weapons, from "tactical battlefield" weapons to strategic nukes, have been so thoroughly integrated into both the weapons systems and the war-fighting doctrines of both sides that there is no way they can wage war against each other without the large-scale employment of nuclear weapons — besides the fact that neither side is at all likely to actually get involved in this war and then turn around and decide that rather than risk the destruction that the introduction of nuclear

[10] See "Nuclear War Fighting With a Certified Dove," *RW*, No. 244 (February 24, 1984), p. 8; "What's So New About Nuclear War," *RW*, No. 248 (March 23, 1984), p. 1; Robert S. McNamara, McGeorge Bundy, et al., "Nuclear Weapons and the Atlantic Alliance," *Foreign Affairs*, Spring 1982, pp. 753-68; and Robert S. McNamara, "The Military Role of Nuclear Weapons: Perceptions and Misperceptions," *Foreign Affairs*, Winter 1983/1984, pp. 59-80. For an analysis of Soviet military doctrine and how it reflects the imperialist nature of the Soviet Union and the attempts of its rulers to be in a position to fight and win a war with the Western imperialist bloc, including the use of nuclear weapons as the decisive force, see Mike Ely, "Against the 'Lesser Evil' Thesis: Soviet Preparations for World War 3," *Revolution*, No. 52 (Summer 1984), pp. 29-55.

weapons would involve, they will simply surrender instead, since conventional war (with perhaps some tactical nuclear weapons) has gone badly for them! Every significant imperialist strategist, the "critics" referred to included, knows that the question they face is how to be in the best position to fight and win if it comes, as it will, to a choice between that and simply letting the other side have clear-cut domination in the world: a choice equally unthinkable — far more unthinkable than nuclear war — to the imperialists on both sides.

In short, it is a deadly error — and deadly is far too weak a word given what the stakes are and what time it is on the clock of world events and world history — to be taken in by the reasonable assurances and pious declarations of the imperialists: they *will* do it, because they have to; they will do it. . .unless they are prevented by revolution.

JFK and RR

The basis, or cause, for the increasingly open belligerent posture of U.S. imperialism and the push from its side toward world war is not "the rise of the right," nor Ronald Reagan personally or the fact that he is in office, and so on. These are effects, symbols, and instruments of a system in profound crisis and approaching the forcible, cataclysmic eruption of its basic contradictions, as well as of the particular position and role of U.S. imperialism in world relations today.

To get at this, a comparison between John F. Kennedy and Ronald Reagan might be helpful. In a couple of the articles in the series *Reflections and Sketches* — in particular "On Phil Ochs, Or Why You Can't Have Kennedy and Revolution Too" and "Frank Sinatra" — I spoke to how the image and rôle of John F. Kennedy was based on a certain position and certain maneuvering room for U.S. imperialism which no longer exist in the same way today.[11] If JFK were alive and chief executive of U.S. im-

[11] "On Phil Ochs, Or Why You Can't Have Kennedy and Revolution Too," *RW*, No. 176 (October 15, 1982), p. 3; "Frank Sinatra," *RW*, No. 182 (November 26, 1982), p. 3.

perialism today his basic orientation and his policies, especially in the crucial arena of international relations and more particularly the confrontation with the rival Soviet bloc, would not only be fundamentally the same as those of Ronald Reagan, but would be very similar in many specifics. In fact (and some bourgeois commentators, particularly more openly right-wing ones, seem to delight in pointing this out) there is a lot more in common between RR and JFK than many people, especially many liberals, would like to acknowledge.

Why does Ronald Reagan uphold, even in large part identify himself with, the legacy of John Kennedy (and he has made a point on a number of occasions of doing so)? Clearly, it can only be for JFK's "tough" stand vis-à-vis the Soviets, in particular around the Cuban Missile Crisis. We have pointed out elsewhere that this Missile Crisis did not lead to and was extremely unlikely to lead to world war. Fundamentally, this was because the rise to power of the new bourgeoisie within the Communist Party of the Soviet Union (headed at that time by Khrushchev) and the restoration of capitalism there led to a situation where the Soviet Union and the bloc it led posed no obstacle *as a socialist camp* to the U.S. bloc, and this new bourgeoisie was unprepared to mount a straight-up challenge to the U.S. and its allies as rival imperialists. It had the necessity instead to seek to collude with U.S. imperialism to suppress revolutions and to compete and contend with U.S. imperialism within a framework of more or less peaceful relations between the two superpowers and the two blocs (that is, avoiding a direct military confrontation at all costs). The Cuban Missile Crisis dramatically established that it was the U.S. that would maintain the upper hand in this situation and that it would be the USSR that would have to do the backing down to avoid world war if push was about to come to shove.

Now, however, world relations and the "world balance of forces" (as the revisionists in the USSR and their followers like to say) have changed sharply, with the result that the question of which side will have the upper hand is precisely the question acutely posed on the agenda. Neither side can afford to back down from a major confrontation with the other — one which would cast the die as to which side will dominate — but is driven to put everything on the line to decide exactly this. Thus it is the "tough stand" of Kennedy against the Russians that Reagan is identifying with and making use of in the current world situation where this can only mean and only serve actually going down with the Russians: world war/nuclear devastation.

And why is it that Reagan also repeatedly identifies himself in many different ways (right down to radio addresses) with another paragon of Democratic Party liberalism, Franklin D. Roosevelt? What is it that he and FDR have in common? Their domestic economic programs? Their specific attitudes and policies in regard to social programs, especially for "the unemployed, the poor, the minorities," etc.? No, obviously not. But there is one fundamental thing in common! (though Reagan *so far* is still preparing for *his* role as commander in chief in a global showdown).

So even while Reagan raves and foams open reaction, he revives the memory (and many "echoes") of FDR for that one thing they have in common (or will, if the U.S. imperialists keep Reagan as President and the advance of the world revolution does not "intervene" to topple the whole agenda). At the same time he also revives the FDR and the JFK images for another very important reason: to make it appear as if this whole thing (moving toward war) is all being done by a reasonable man, and reluctantly — responsibly and with agonizing, as we are told JFK agonized as he risked the fate of humanity to ensure that the USSR could not have missiles ninety miles from the U.S. border while the U.S. had them much closer to the Soviet border (in Turkey, for example). This image of the reasonable, responsible (even agonizing) man at the helm as the "ship of state" heads into the "winds of war" is especially important for Ronald Reagan (and the whole U.S. ruling class), given Reagan's other tough-guy, gunslinger "track."

The example of how JFK handled the Cuban Missile Crisis — or rather, the image and mythology that has been created around this — is employed now in the service of soothing people and seducing them into believing that if (and only if) we have someone with the nerve to go "eyeball to eyeball" with the Russians "without blinking," it will be possible to avoid a war with them, with all its disastrous consequences. (Another example where this basic logic was sharply presented: on American TV, ABC's "Crisis Game." It was not by any accident, I believe, that this "Crisis Game" — with its message that war with the Russians can be avoided only if "we" responsibly but firmly stand up to them — followed immediately after *The Day After.* Anyone who thinks that was an accident — or doesn't even know about this "Crisis Game" program — needs the waking up that we're talking about.) All this is precisely not for the purpose of avoiding war with the rival Soviet-led bloc but of preparing (people) *for* just this war.

What all this shows, from several different angles, is that fundamentally it is not "the man at the helm" who determines monumental questions like this (world war/nuclear devastation) but the imperialist system and "the times" — the compulsion of that system, the interests of and demands on the imperialist ruling class flowing from that compulsion in the context of the actual world relations. And there is not one of their politicians of any significance — *not one* — who would give a different answer than Ronald Reagan (or for that matter JFK or FDR before him) to the basic question: which is preferable, world war/nuclear devastation or the U.S. reduced to not being "number one"?[12] That is exactly the question the U.S. imperialists and all their major politicians are facing. And you only have to listen to them with a discerning ear to know their answer

[12] This basic orientation is well captured in Ken Follett's novel about intrigue surrounding the Russo-English alliance at the start of World War 1, *The Man From St. Petersburg* (New York: Signet, 1983). The English Lord Walden charged with cementing this alliance several times protests that he does not *want* war with all its carnage and suffering, *but* he is clear that such a war is preferable to seeing Germany supplant England as dominant world power. Today, while a world war would bring carnage and suffering on a whole other level beyond even the horrors of the previous two world wars, the position of the ruling "lords" of all the imperialist powers remains — and can only remain under such a system — that such a war is preferable to seeing "the other side" have dominance in the world.

to it: nothing could be more unthinkable than for the U.S. to be reduced to "second class status" in the world (to say nothing of the U.S. suffering a totally devastating military defeat, or even worse being overthrown by revolution); for them this is a far worse horror than the world and the mass of humanity being devastated by world war and nuclear destruction.

Imperialist Chauvinistic Fatalism and World War 3

> *"Everybody wants to go to heaven but nobody wants to die."* — *Peter Tosh*

In "World War Must Be Opposed With Revolution, Not Peace" I referred to what I called "a kind of fatalistic nationalist sentiment that arises among the oppressed peoples and nations" and "finds expression in the notion that if the imperialists blow each other up and destroy much of their own homelands, so be it and perhaps the world will even be better off as a result."[13] This is an important phenomenon and a tendency to be combated, but much worse and of much greater significance is the problem of the chauvinism of much of the masses — and frankly much of the "peace movement" — in the imperialist countries. This includes the fairly widespread notion that (as it was put in the article referred to just above) "all would be right with the world if only world war, especially major battles and nuclear exchanges, can be avoided in these countries" and that the daily suffering of the mass of people in the Third World can "just go on as it is, or at least must not be opposed in such a way as to drag the 'advanced' countries into a devastating conflagration."

Another important form of this chauvinism is what could

[13] "World War Must Be Opposed With Revolution," *RW*, No. 227, p. 3. See also "Provocations," *RW*, No. 228 (October 28, 1983), p. 3.

be called "imperialist chauvinistic fatalism." This finds expression especially among the middle classes and generally the more privileged strata of the population in the imperialist countries who often are aware, sometimes even acutely aware, of the real danger and the very real horror of world war/nuclear devastation but nonetheless say, "what can you do about it?" What the real meaning of that fatalistic sentiment comes down to is that it's not worth really disrupting your life, taking any real risks, stepping out of line or going out on a limb to try to really do what's necessary to oppose this at its source and have any real chance of preventing it. In many ways these people are like Jackson Browne's "Lawyers in Love": ". . . Tuned in to 'Happy Days'/waiting for World War 3 . . ." and even in some cases willing to see the Soviets nuked out of existence if that could, somehow, solve the problem without any damage to the U.S. and disruption of their privileged existence (and perhaps even allow them to have "the USSR open soon as vacationland for lawyers in love").

This imperialist chauvinistic fatalism must be exposed and struggled sharply against. But more fundamentally, it shows why these strata — even the active antiwar, antinuke forces among them — can't be relied on as any kind of basic force to deal with these questions and specifically to see the fight through to prevent world war, whatever it takes. They don't have — and left to themselves can't and won't come to — the answer, the solution to all this, nor the strength and resoluteness to carry it through with their own efforts. Many among these strata can, however, be won and mobilized by a strong movement of the basic masses behind a proletarian revolutionary and internationalist line — which is the only force and the only line that can provide the necessary direction and fundamental resolution (a point to be returned to later).

The Day the Earth Stood Still

In the article "More Questions to Carl Sagan, Stephen Gould, and Isaac Asimov,"[14] in the series *More Reflections and Sketches*, I spoke to the effort to avert nuclear war and its disastrous consequences through attempting to prove — not only to the people at large but in particular to the powers-that-be in the respective countries — that such a war would be irrational from the vantage point of humanity's interests, indeed its very survival. I pointed out that, however powerfully such arguments may be made and supporting facts marshaled, this approach is bound to fail, because in a world dominated by imperialism and marked by class oppression, the division between oppressor and oppressed nations, and the rivalry of imperialist marauders — all resting on a foundation of capitalist commodity production — there is no way for the interests of humanity as a whole to be fully grasped, let alone acted upon — except through the world revolutionary movement of the proletariat to overthrow, overcome, and uproot all this.

The desire and attempt to prevent nuclear war through reasoned appeals to the general and higher interests of the human species definitely has its positive side — although, unfortunately, most who voice such appeals are not completely consistent or thoroughgoing in their opposition to war preparations, and try to combine their opposition with patriotism or "refined" patriotism and haven't really ruptured with the outlook of "my country first or above all" even while being genuinely concerned with humanity's fate. This, together with the failure to really reckon with the actual relations and divisions in the world and the underlying material-economic basis for this, means that such an approach is bound not only to fail but, whatever the intention may be, to spread confusion and demoralization; and, if it remains on this level, it will ultimately work against the monumental struggle to prevent war.

To put it another way, there is not going to be divine nor even interplanetary intervention to prevent such a war: no *Day*

[14] "More Questions to Carl Sagan, Stephen Gould, and Isaac Asimov," *RW*, No. 207 (May 27, 1983), p. 3.

the Earth Stood Still. The approach of appealing to reason and the general (and classless) interests of humanity would, to be effective, have to be addressed to and rely on what does not exist: a rational will divorced from and standing above human social and world relations. But it seems that, instead of waiting for divine or interplanetary intervention, it is more realistic to address our appeals and our political efforts to mobilizing the masses of people throughout the world, including in the U.S. and other imperialist countries, to rise in revolution to sweep away the existing social and world relations and establish new ones that are not in fundamental conflict with the interests of the great majority of humanity and indeed of humanity as a whole. Which, after all then, is a more realistic prospect: "the day the earth stood still," or the time it witnessed a new and radical, a truly unprecedented, revolution right here on earth?

The "Fram Oil Filter" Line

This refers to the Fram oil filter ad (from several years ago), with its slogan: "pay me now [for an oil filter — a comparatively minor cost] or pay me later [for a complete overhaul of a ruined engine]."

Here it's relevant to recall the argument made by Carl Sagan that serious reduction of nuclear weapons and other arms control measures would make a real difference, because even if world war could not be altogether prevented there is still a world of difference between a relatively "small" nuclear exchange (say of a few dozen nuclear weapons fired by each side) and the kind of much more massive exchange that would bring on the "nuclear winter" that Sagan has been urgently warning about. While Sagan's concerns are certainly real, he is fundamentally wrong in terms of the possibility of preventing massive nuclear destruction through arms limitations; but his insistence on the qualitative differences in levels of destruction points to an important lesson, different from the one he intended.

Given that, in fact, arms control, reductions, etc., are illusory as a solution to the danger of nuclear devastation (for all the reasons touched on earlier), there is an analogy with the Fram oil filter line in this sense: worldwide upheaval and revolutionary warfare, including civil war in the U.S. itself, does not imply the same destruction as world war and major nuclear exchanges between the two imperialist blocs. And we (the communist vanguard, uniting around the banner and *Declaration* of the Revolutionary Internationalist Movement, the revolutionary forces of the international proletariat and oppressed masses throughout the world) will be around anyway to make revolution *even if* that means doing so during or in the aftermath of such a world war — in which case at least a part of our forces will survive and continue to wage revolutionary war against counterrevolutionary war with the aim of delivering a shattering defeat to the reactionary forces and preventing them from regrouping and reorganizing the world (or what's left of it) under their domination and starting the whole thing going yet again.

We will be around for such a struggle, if that's what it comes to, just as the imperialists are *already planning* to be around to enforce their social system and values, *even after* all that it will have led to (they sound insane in this, but that is indeed what they intend to do and there is a certain logic to it — the same logic that will lead to world war unless it is prevented by revolution). So, "pay us now or pay us later": join with us now in the struggle to make proletarian revolution and prevent world war in that way — the *only way* it can in fact be prevented — or wait and face the prospect of joining with those of our forces that do remain and are continuing to wage the revolutionary struggle against the forces of the imperialists *during and in the aftermath* of world war with all its devastation.

If the accusation is made that it sounds "mercenary," "cold," etc., to address such a message to those it is intended for — in particular, middle-class people and generally the privileged strata in the imperialist countries — let's recall that it is not we who say (in deed if not in word) that it is preferable to let world war happen (with all that means) rather than risk losing such a privileged position and putting everything on the line to prevent it — whatever it takes. So, with such people in mind especially, I repeat: "pay us now or pay us later."

The Baretta TV Show Theme

This was expressed in the refrain of the show's theme song — "don't do the crime if you can't do the time" — with its meaning: don't pull stick-ups, assaults, and so on if you aren't prepared to pay the price (go to jail — do the time); don't get into all this without thinking about where it might all lead.

Here I apply basically the same principle to say to all those who take the benefits — their share in the spoils — from imperialist exploitation and plunder worldwide and who defend this system and what it does to people all over the world, knowing (on one level or another) that this is the basis for their privileged position: Be aware that constant upheaval, revolutionary struggles and uprising against this system and the existing conditions and relations, armed confrontation between revolution and counterrevolution as well as between imperialist rivals, which are all coming to a head now; the imminent possibility of world war with all its destruction and desolation and at the same time heightened revolutionary upheaval and revolutionary warfare — all this is where the contradictions of this system and its inner motion and logic are leading you along with everyone else in the world. This, all this, is what it means to live under the imperialist system, even with a position of comparative privilege. And, on top of all this, for those who choose to go down with the imperialist system, there will be that further price to pay. So: "Don't do the crime if you can't do the time."

World War, Nuclear Destruction, and Lopsidedness

In *Conquer the World* the phenomenon of lopsidedness is explained in basic terms: the concentration of the advanced productive forces in a handful of imperialist countries exploiting and feasting parasitically off the world and in particular the colonial (or neocolonial) and dependent countries, where in most cases there are only small islands of advanced areas within a sea of backward social conditions and relations and where the overall economy is extremely disarticulated while the masses suffer brutal exploitation, oppression, and poverty. Thus the desire of the masses for revolution and the possibilities for revolution are generally more favorable where the productive forces and conditions generally are backward, while revolutionary prospects are generally less favorable where the productive forces are more advanced.[15] A particular, concentrated, and monstrous expression of all this: nuclear weapons are overwhelmingly in the hands of and controlled by those countries where conditions for revolution are generally less favorable and where even with the approach of this world-historic conjuncture revolutionary situations have not yet come into existence — and the ruling classes of these countries impose on the world and the mass of humanity the constant blackmail of these weapons and now the growing, imminent threat of their actual use, on a large scale.

This is another sharp (and grotesque) expression of why the struggle against nuclear war must have as its driving and leading force the revolutionary struggle against imperialism and why it must be a truly global struggle and based on internationalism — and specifically the thoroughly revolutionary internationalism of the proletariat, for whom world war represents the greatest crime but certainly not the only great crime of imperialism, a concentration and magnification of the daily horrors of life and death under this system, not an exception to or aberration from an otherwise tolerable situation.

[15] Bob Avakian, *Conquer the World? The International Proletariat Must and Will*, published as *Revolution*, No. 50 (December 1981), especially pp. 36-38. These points are further elaborated on not only in *Conquer the World*, but more fully in *America in Decline*, Vol. 1.

What We Intend to Do With the Productive Forces

We have seen where the domination by the imperialists of the world's productive forces (including the mass of people who create technology through their labor) has led, and especially where it is leading now: toward world war. Once having recognized this, the vision of utilizing the productive forces in a dramatically different, diametrically opposed way becomes all the more compelling.

If revolution does succeed in preventing world war, then speaking not only of the general orientation of the international proletariat and its communist vanguard but specifically of (what is now) the U.S.: at whatever time power is seized by the proletariat, and whatever the immediate conditions in the country might be, *from the beginning* this lopsidedness must be systematically attacked, even with the significant sacrifices this will involve, including for the basic masses in the country. Or else it will be back before long to the same system that was overthrown and all its truly monstrous crimes once again. (And this principle has especially important application for not only the U.S. but for — the formerly — imperialist countries in general, as and whenever power is seized there.) If, on the other hand, revolution does not succeed in preventing world war, our basic orientation must remain that of proceeding first and above all from the perspective of transforming the whole world and rebuilding from the start on the basis of seeking not to reestablish but to overcome any such lopsidedness. Therefore, we openly declare — and even now must do more to create public opinion around — what we intend to do with the productive forces, under whatever conditions exist when we come to control them: above all to utilize them to promote revolution and the complete remaking of the world and its previously dominant conditions, relations, and divisions, continuing the advance to achieve the goal of a communist world, where the lopsided character of today's world will have been overcome, the division of oppressor and oppressed nations and the division of society into classes will have been eliminated, and the soil for all these thoroughly uprooted in every sphere.

"Maoism," "Primitive Communism," and the "Theory of the Productive Forces"

The caricature of Maoism and of Mao's line is that of trying to impose an idealistic vision of communism — which would amount to a primitive communism — on an unwilling world and unwilling people; this, it is said, is the reason why it was bound to fail and did fail. As opposed to this, Mao's actual line on the transition to communism is based on the continuation of classes and class struggle and the need for the continuation of the revolution under the dictatorship of the proletariat, both because of the conditions within China (and this applies to socialist countries generally, owing to the long-term persistence of bourgeois right and other remnants of capitalism in socialist society) and because of the fact that communist society can only be achieved on a world scale. On this basis, Mao fought for the orientation of "grasp revolution, promote production" and of taking the struggle of the socialist road versus the capitalist road as the central problem — including making great sacrifices for the advance of the world revolution (for example, extending aid to Vietnam for many years until the Soviet Union clearly established its dominance there in the mid-'70s). All this is in direct and fundamental opposition to the "theory of the productive forces" which insists that proletarian revolution and socialist transformation are only possible where technology and culture are most highly developed and that the main task, once the old ruling class is overthrown, is to develop technology and production technique (this is the line of the revisionists, including those now ruling China).

Here it is important to discuss how the basic Maoist orientation would apply if revolution does not advance far enough, fast enough to prevent world war. In such a situation it will be the task of the proletariat to wage revolutionary warfare to seize power wherever possible during and even in the aftermath of such a war (and here I am reminded of my perhaps appropriately apocalyptic comments on this in a 1979 speech at a forum in Seattle — that we would still have to and would wage revolutionary struggle even if only 500 people were left in the world in the aftermath of nuclear destruction). And there will be fierce struggle, even in the aftermath of such a war, over what social system, what relations and values will be established and be in command. It would be better — far better — in such conditions to start on the basis of a kind of primitive communism and go forward from there to reconstitute and rebuild toward a fully communist world than to accept the division of society yet again into a system of class division, exploitation, and oppression.[16]

Such an orientation — of fighting to begin society on a primitive communist basis and rebuild from that in a way to advance toward a fully communist world, in the aftermath of world war and nuclear devastation — is not idealist but would represent the only real alternative to the compounded horror of having such a war and devastation only to find the same social system, relations, and values once more dominating the world, with all too familiar consequences and leading toward all too predictable a future! While, in such "aftermath conditions," all kinds of brutal tendencies and cutthroat pressures would be set loose and nurtured, there would still be a basis to overcome this, and humanity would not have lost all its historically accumulated knowledge. What Lenin wrote at the closing stages of World War 1 remains true despite the fact that World War 3 would bring qualitatively greater destruction to the entire globe:

[16] Science fiction writer Ursula LeGuin in her book *The Dispossessed* (New York: Avon, 1974) grapples with the problem of beginning "from scratch" with a classless society on a foundation of economic backwardness but with a high degree of social consciousness and technological knowledge. To accentuate the point she has this society begun on a new planet by self-exiles from their native planet — which is very similar to human society on this earth as we know it. Despite the fact that hers is not a Marxist-Leninist outlook, there are many provocative insights and a real grappling with profound questions in this book.

"For no matter to what extent culture has been destroyed, it cannot be removed from history; it will be difficult to restore but no destruction will ever mean the complete disappearance of that culture."[17]

Whether or not revolution is able to prevent world war or occurs during or only in the aftermath of that war, it will be a question of ferocious struggle to determine under what social system, what relations, and guided by what values, toward what end, this culture (the accumulated knowledge and ability to transform nature acquired by humanity up to now) will be utilized. Far better primitive communism than the foundation of imperialism as a starting point in the aftermath of nuclear destruction, if it comes to that.

Imperialism — No Future; But What About the Future of Humanity?

The imperialist system — as it now exists, West and East — is through: either its whole framework will be shattered by revolution, forcing a whole new world realignment sufficient to prevent world war, or this world war will occur and will destroy much of human civilization and the present imperialist framework along with it (and this is qualitatively beyond the situation of the two previous world wars, whose outcome was bound to and did witness a major restructuring of world relations). This does not mean that it is impossible for the imperialist system as such to survive this world war, for new imperialist forces or new dominant exploiting states to emerge (or even for some kind of reorganization to occur in part at least under presently existing imperialist forces); but as it now exists, East and West, the imperialist world has no future.

But what about the future of humanity? Any possible

[17] V.I. Lenin, "Extraordinary Seventh Congress of the R.C.P.(B.), (March 6-8, 1918)," *Collected Works* (*LCW*) (Moscow: Progress Publishers, 1977), Vol. 27, p. 129.

future besides the devastation of nuclear war — and on a different path than what produces such a horrendous thing — is and can only be proletarian revolution and the future of communism. In any event, given what is before us, it will not be possible to avoid tremendous sacrifice and even significant destruction. As I wrote in "World War Must Be Opposed With Revolution, Not Peace":

> In the period ahead, with the gathering and exploding of the world contradictions of the imperialist system, it will not be possible, nor desirable, to avoid tremendous upheaval and radical ruptures in world relations and in many societies, nor can all this change come about any way except violently. But it may be possible to prevent through revolution a world war which would be senseless carnage and destruction of the greatest magnitude, unprecedented bloodletting and devastation solely in the interests of perpetuating the very system that has produced such a monstrosity, along with all the other evils deriving from and characteristic of such a system, and solely to determine which set of plunderers would preside over and gorge themselves on the aftermath.[18]

To be a part of the genuinely world-historic struggle to prevent this and to fight for another, radically different future for humanity — the future of communism — in the face of whatever monstrous crimes imperialism is able to commit before it is swept from the earth: this remains in all cases the only goal which, in the final analysis, is worth living, and dying, for.

[18] "World War Must Be Opposed With Revolution," *RW*, No. 227, p. 4.

QUESTIONS CONCERNING REVOLUTIONARY POSSIBILITIES

The '80s: Decade of Extremes

Both sides, worldwide — the imperialists and reactionaries of both blocs on the one side, the proletariat and revolutionary masses on the other — will be faced with the need to seek extreme solutions to extreme circumstances. The '80s is not the '60s, true enough — but still less is it (will it be) the '50s! (One reflection of this, in the cultural sphere: the attempts of the U.S. ruling class to revive some of the values and norms, including fashions, styles, etc., of the '50s, is partial, modified. It is mixed with some revival of the '40s, i.e., wartime conditions!, but more with the conditions and "atmosphere," in particular the desperate decadent edge, of the '80s.) This is not a period coming off but one leading toward a major explosion of the world contradictions of the imperialist system and toward a resolution (one way or the other, on one level or another) of these contradictions through forcible and highly destructive means.

There is and will increasingly be sharp polarization in society. Although this will involve contradiction and spiral-like and not straight-line motion, the "middle ground" will be increasingly shrinking and the position of conciliation characteristic of the middle forces will be undermined as things come to a head. In the '60s in the U.S., while there were real and powerful revolutionary trends, there was still for most the underlying assumption that there was plenty of material abundance to go around, and even among the most oppressed in rebellion there was an aspect of "everybody else is doing okay and getting theirs — and I want mine!" Things in the '80s already are and will even more dramatically be on a far different foundation than this.

All this is a *good* thing — not something to shrink from or be intimidated by — but it requires the revolutionary outlook of the proletariat, a radical rupture with the present system and its values, to grasp this, to even recognize let alone seize the opportunities amidst the extreme circumstances.

"Revolutions Gone Sour"

Some sharp examples: China follows, within two decades, down the same path of capitalist restoration as the Soviet Union and there are no longer any socialist states at this time; Iran and Nicaragua give inspiration (especially coming only a few years after the loss in China) but, while certain reactionary class forces were overthrown and some blows struck at imperialism, no fundamental change, no real liberation occurred — no real rupture with imperialist world relations and real embarking on the socialist road — and instead new exploiting class forces (of one type or another) imposed their rule as new compradors dependent on and serving imperialism while maintaining "revolutionary" pretensions in one form or another.

These setbacks are part of the motion toward the approaching world-historic conjuncture and not "the end of the story" (even for the revolution in those countries but most of all for the world revolutionary movement) for this period.

During this "approach" to that conjuncture, in many ways things are more unfavorable for the proletariat than when everything does come much more fully to (or even further toward) the exploding point. The imperialists and reactionaries have more maneuvering room than they will have when things become even more intense, are "drawn tight"...explode.

A correct understanding of such setbacks, recognizing that they are bound up with the overall world situation and its motion and development — not merely the general historical context of the world struggle between imperialism and the forces of proletarian revolution but the specific, immediate world situation and where it is headed — such an understanding is essential in order to fully learn from this negative experience, and specifically to grasp the heightened revolutionary opportunities the approaching conjuncture holds.

The Prince "1999" Line

This "line," especially in its desperate edge, does express the sentiments of significant sections of the masses, especially many youth, including proletarian youth. I find interesting the constant and very sharp tension (at least in the one Prince album that I've been able to listen to, "1999") between the general sort of nihilistic hedonism that runs through it and the underlying and sometimes surfacing sense that something is wrong with this and it is not going to work after all. This is true also of the title song "1999": They're going to blow the world up; my mind says fight but deep down I know there's nothing that can be done about it, so let's party, "I'm gonna listen to my body tonight."

It's important to talk about this line and specifically why it won't make it, including, ironically, on its own terms (and here the comment of a friend upon listening to this Prince album is very insightful: "to these people partying is deadly serious business"). It's impossible to get real satisfaction with all this shit surrounding you and hanging over your head and impossible to avoid being drawn into the "vortex" of gathering world events — impossible exactly because of what time it is and what is up (note that "1999" even speaks to this, especially in its ending — "Mommy, why does everybody have a bomb . . . mommy, why does everybody have a bomb?").

Such a line is an expression of particular features of the immediate situation — including that there is no powerful proletarian revolutionary movement yet to sweep masses of people in (in the U.S. or generally on the international plane). There *are*, however, crucial developments that hold this potential: above all the Revolutionary Internationalist Movement but other "shoots" as well, in particular the revolutionary war in Peru actually led by a communist vanguard participating in the Revolutionary Internationalist Movement and the existence of other steeled vanguard parties (also participating in the Revolutionary Internationalist Movement), including our party in the U.S., heading into the real "1999" — in the '80s.

Some Straight Talk on the Possibilities for Proletarian Revolution in the U.S.

It really is true that the whole world will be radically transformed in any case — one way or the other — in the next few years. You can't look at the question of proletarian revolution in static terms: as if there will be major upheavals in the world, in which the U.S. will be deeply enmeshed, but somehow things and people will stay basically the same throughout all this — *that* is totally unrealistic, impossible.

Yes, in one sense we are "playing a long shot" but it's "our best shot." And, from a world-historic standpoint — or even viewing things in terms of what the U.S. and other imperialists are confronted with — *their* position is more difficult, more desperate (keeping in mind what was said earlier about the future of imperialism as it exists today — that it is finished as such — versus the question of the future of humanity).

They are not invincible — they are not all that "bad," strategically (check out Vietnam, for example — a deep wound they have not recovered from completely, by any means). And once things get to the point where we can make an initial breakthrough strong enough and keep it going long enough to shatter their traditional methods of suppression by force, then it's a whole new deal. (*That*, "quiet as it's kept," is *not* totally unrealistic, impossible — which I'll come back to shortly.)

We do after all have a party that actually is undertaking all its work to prepare itself and especially the advanced among the masses now for exactly this situation, a party that has the ability to seriously approach such an armed struggle — first of all the understanding and the correct outlook and methodology, and therefore also the basis to develop the appropriate organizational expression given the circumstances (this is not jive or selling wolf-tickets but a matter of serious all-around preparation).

The Positive and Negative of Impatience

It is right to be impatient — impatient for revolution. But to the degree that this is an expression of and means political paralysis, it is not good — and works against revolution.

The fact that our party, with our clear, firm orientation of undertaking everything we do as part of the overall preparation for the armed struggle to overthrow imperialism — the fact that we are *not* right now attempting to launch that armed struggle shows (perhaps ironically) how serious we really are: serious about winning! When things ripen more, when we can make a real go at it, then we must do so — and we must have prepared to do so — all-out and with the orientation, plans, strategy, and tactics to make it real: with the real intent to fight through and *win.*

Again On How Political Preparation Is Key Now

What do we mean by such preparation? Here it is necessary to summarize a few basic points:

The central task of our party — create public opinion/seize power — is (or comprehends) an overall process, so that the seeds of, or elements of, seizing power are present and must be nurtured and developed even in today's circumstances where the ongoing focus is creating public opinion in an all-around way for proletarian revolution.

Exposure — bringing to light the nature and features of the enemy and of other classes and social groupings and forces, in an all-around way, from many different angles and following close on major social questions and world events — is the key link now in carrying out the central task.

Supporting the outbreaks of protest and rebellion of the

masses — above all by "stretching the proletarian revolutionary line into them" but also by entering more fully into the arenas of serious struggle and confrontation between masses of people and the imperialists and giving even greater emphasis to leading especially the advanced among the basic masses to mount the political stage, under the banner of the revolutionary proletariat (of the party and of the Revolutionary Internationalist Movement in particular) — as stressed in our party's last Central Committee Report, this is of increased importance in today's situation.[19]

The party's newspaper is central to all this and the main weapon to be wielded now, in preparation for the future.

Without such political preparation it is impossible to develop a really thoroughgoing revolutionary position, and instead one will be fooled and turned back into the fold of the enemy in one form or another. Such political preparation is absolutely necessary in order to be able to identify, expose, isolate, and break the political hold of those whose special role it is to channel the growing unrest and erupting anger of the masses of oppressed into "approved" and "safe" outlets, especially at crucial moments of acute crisis, and who are now carrying out *their* active preparation for this with the full support of the ruling class (people like Jesse Jackson, for example).

Without such political preparation the advanced revolutionary-minded forces (including the party itself) will almost certainly fail even to recognize the revolutionary opportunity — the acute crisis and the deep crack in the ruling structure that provide the necessary and long-awaited opening.

Such political preparation is the most important way to influence the political terrain now, to plant and nurture the seeds and shoots of a future armed uprising, to learn more fully the features of the enemy and all classes and strata in society, and to develop — especially among the advanced, with the party at the

[19] *Accumulating Revolutionary Forces for the Coming Showdown*, Report from the 1982 Central Committee of the RCP,USA, with "Background Material," printed as a supplement in *RW*, No. 194 (February 25, 1983).

core — the political ability and "maturity" to handle the extremely complex, tortuous, and magnified character of the revolutionary situation, when it does ripen, and of the actual revolutionary armed struggle for power.

Politics and Politics

As the U.S. imperialists most often define it — and seek to confine it — politics is the contest, within their own ranks or at least on their own terms, involving contradictions between the interests of individuals (or segments of society, and segments of the ruling class in particular) and the overall interests of the ruling class as a whole. Such politics means the contest to hold office (elections), the conflict of "special interests" versus the "general good" (the general interests of the ruling class), etc.; "bringing in politics" or "making something a political issue" means bringing in personal or particular aims or interests, in opposition to the general interest (as just defined).[20] It is hardly accidental that such a defining (and confining) of politics leaves out such "minor details" as the division of society into oppressor and oppressed classes and nations — fundamental conditions in society at this stage, the recognition of which is essential for even beginning to have a correct understanding of politics.

For the proletariat, and in reality, politics is the struggle to influence and change society. In the era of human history in which society is divided into classes this finds its most basic and essential expression in class struggle. In accordance with this, it is of crucial importance for the class-conscious proletariat to mount the political stage, in every important arena and dimen-

[20] The recently published book, *The Media Monopoly*, by Ben Bagdikian (New York: Beacon Press, 1983), is a good example of this. It does contain some interesting exposure of the control and manipulation of the media by large corporations and it has stirred some controversy, but it presents the fundamental conflict as the attempt of such corporations to pursue and serve their own "private" interests against the general good; this places the problem squarely within the confines of bourgeois democracy — and bourgeois rule.

sion, and contest with the ruling class and its major representatives, of all various stripes, over the major social questions and world events — all in preparation for carrying the class struggle over to its highest form, the armed struggle for political power, as soon as possible.

In today's world especially, it would be a disaster if the ruling class and its representatives succeeded in containing the awakening and activism of oppressed masses within the arena of politics as the bourgeoisie defines, confines, and controls it. But it would also be a disaster if especially the advanced among the proletariat did not enter into that decisive arena of what politics *really* is — especially now. Of course the bourgeoisie does on occasion use politics in another, more general sense — and then generally in a negative sense, to denote "bad politics": opposition to the established order, or order as they are determined to establish it. Then we hear the cry against "bringing in politics" in a larger dimension, for example, the *1968*, or *1984* Olympics — as opposed to 1980. In this sense we must give them much more of such "bad politics" — working toward doing so in its highest form as soon as possible!

Co-optation in the '80s

The ruling class is paying great attention to this now — promoting "heroes" and "models," especially from among the oppressed nationalities (as in Ronald Reagan's 1984 "State of the Union Address"), and promoting lures that seem within the reach of the masses, not just "pots of gold" in some far-off and alien realm (for example, millions of youth can see themselves breakdancing — not to put it down as such or ignore its positive side, but on the other hand the ruling class has "moved in on it" quickly). And of course this last period has been the year of the Black Everything — the Black Astronaut, Black Miss America (even two of them). . .and oh yes the Black Presidential Candidate. All this even though — or more to the point, *because* — there are millions and millions of people among the basic masses who are not only poor but desperate. And for many among the basic masses conditions generally are worse than at any time since the last world war. A new world war coming on the agenda now is just the point and just what the ruling class has as its hole card in all its co-optation, "you can make it, it's up to you" hype.

The actual material conditions — including the fact that the basis for "upward mobility" is actually being undermined for the oppressed masses (as opposed to a few individuals "elevated" out of the mass to be held up as "models") — these material conditions are growing more favorable for the revolutionary proletariat (while they are strategically unfavorable for the reformist peddlers of conciliation with this monstrous system and the "you can make it if you try" pimps). But this means all the more that the revolutionary proletarian pole — with the party at the core — must be out there as a powerful force on the political stage, influencing the political terrain, with a clear-cut and uncompromising revolutionary stand and program; or else disillusionment with the lure of "upward mobility" will lead to cynicism and other sentiments that play into the hands of and serve the ruling class and lead the victims right back into the "killing embrace" of that ruling class.

Present Conditions and Political Suffocation

On the one hand the increasingly difficult, even desperate situation for millions of the basic masses weighs down on them and demoralizes many, forcing them to be preoccupied with the struggle just to keep things together, "body and soul," on a minimal level — for a growing number "survival" is not a catchword for eating others alive to "make it" but a real life-and-death, sanity-and-insanity question.[21]

On the other hand the recognition that most people in the

[21] A powerful expression of this is the rap song "New York, New York" by Grand Master Flash.

U.S. are not in such a situation now and don't favor or gravitate yet toward a radical solution — or, the most visible gravitation toward a radical solution (owing to the promotion of the ruling class) is a gravitation of many demoralized, disoriented, parasitic strata among the middle classes (and privileged workers) toward the radical right — all this also weighs down on even the more politically aware and advanced among the basic masses and holds many back from rallying to the revolutionary banner and mounting the political stage to exert a revolutionary political force. This is also one of the factors holding back many among the basic masses from engaging even in spontaneous acts of rebellion (note how the recent Miami rebellions have been an exception). Add to this the fact that, while there are certain tactical disagreements apparent among the ruling class, there are not any serious, deepgoing splits among them, and all this leads to no small amount of political suffocation — to go along with outright suppression by force — of the basic masses.

This is not a new phenomenon. Lenin referred to how the "burning necessity to mete out summary justice to the bourgeoisie and its servitors who ill-use the people" is held in check by the masses' understanding that "the hour for the serious revolutionary struggle of the people has not yet struck, that the political situation is not ripe for it."[22] And in *Red Papers 4* (theoretical publication of the Revolutionary Union, the forerunner of our party), this same general phenomenon is referred to in terms of how it holds back the masses of Black people from getting into a showdown with the forces of the state — that is, all-out revolutionary struggle for power. But in addition there is something to learn from the negative experience within the international communist movement historically, as well as within the brief history of our party, on this point.

In making the general point quoted above, Lenin drew specifically from the experience of the German Social-Democratic movement at that time which, it turned out, became increasingly revisionist and sapped the revolutionary hatred and energy of

[22] Lenin, "Should We Organize the Revolution?", *LCW*, Vol. 8, p. 172.

the workers by channeling them onto reformist paths. And while in the polemics against adventurism (reprinted in *Red Papers 4*) our position was fundamentally correct — and specifically correct in rejecting the disastrous notion of launching the armed struggle for power right then as a protracted urban guerrilla war in the U.S. — there was also, secondarily, the tendency to put the armed struggle off into a virtual never-never land. There was not enough of an orientation of seeking, even while the form of struggle is not military, to nurture in that struggle the political seeds and elements of the future armed struggle, including by finding the concrete ways to give more politically conscious and clear-cut expression to the spontaneous rebellions and uprisings of the masses that inevitably occur in such a period of political preparation. (There is the negative experience of the Black Panther Party here, too, which, despite its overall revolutionary character, fell into attempting to suppress spontaneous rebellion in the name of giving an organized character to the masses' struggle and ended up only stifling the outrage and energy of the masses that was unleashed in spontaneous rebellion.) Handling this correctly (along the lines indicated above) is itself an important part of creating the most favorable conditions for the masses, including the advanced, to mount the political stage and exert the most powerful force and influence on the political terrain in preparation for the future armed uprising.

What About the Fact that Most People Are Not Politically Active Now?

This is not all bad — since it is part of an overall political picture where the majority don't enthusiastically or actively support either side (us or the imperialist ruling class). As Mao Tsetung perceptively noted: "I believe it is true everywhere that people at the two poles are few while those in the middle are many."[23] Nor

[23] Mao Tsetung, "Talks at a Conference of Secretaries of Provincial, Municipal and Autonomous Region Party Committees," *Selected Works* (*MSW*) (Peking: Foreign Languages Press, 1977). Vol. 5, p. 375. (References to *Selected Works* Volumes 1-4 are from 1967 printings.)

is this fact (that most people are not now politically active) decisive, since this will inevitably change as things sharpen and polarize more — though it is important to keep in mind that, even as the middle ground is being undercut with this further sharpening and polarization, many in the middle will continue to oscillate between the "two poles" (the two sides) and vacillate in their stand.

Those who stand firmly with the revolutionary position will (as Mao's statement above suggests) always be in the minority. And in nonrevolutionary times — including situations where there is serious crisis and the conditions for some are desperate, but an acute crisis making possible real, full revolutionary struggle has not yet emerged — those who desire revolution (or radical change in a general sense) are also bound to be a minority. But as things sharpen further, and especially as they approach a revolutionary crisis, such a minority can exert tremendous influence, far beyond its numbers. This is still more the case as a revolutionary situation actually does emerge and this minority is able to break through the cracks and fissures in society and its ruling apparatus and make a real bid for power.

This is a point referred to in "A Message on Hearing 'The Message'" and "The 'City Game' — and the City, No Game" in *More Reflections and Sketches.*[24] It is a gigantic, liberating truth that the ruling class is desperate to keep that revolutionary minority and its potential supporters from really understanding and acting on! It is also a basic lesson of all revolutions, including the two great proletarian revolutions so far — in Russia and, in a different, more protracted way, in China: in both cases, though there were different circumstances there was a basic similarity where a regime was first established through armed struggle in *part* of the country, involving only a *part* of the people as a whole, giving impetus to civil war in which political power was won throughout the country. In the concrete economic and

[24] "A Message on Hearing 'The Message,'" *RW*, No. 200 (April 8, 1983), p. 3; "The 'City Game' — and the City, No Game," *RW*, No. 201 (April 15, 1983), p. 3.

political conditions of the U.S., this means that once there is a decent chance of coordinating uprisings of the basic masses concentrated in the urban areas into a general armed insurrection which can seize power at least in a number of the major cities and quickly advance from that initial breakthrough, we will have a real fighting chance to swing over many of the middle forces and to actually win. (The implications of this in terms of basic military theory and strategic orientation will be taken up in the discussion on "Questions Concerning the Actual Struggle for Power.")

All this is very much bound up with, indeed fundamentally determined by, the development of the objective world situation and the struggle internationally between the forces of revolution and counterrevolution. This situation, and what it holds, is strategically unfavorable to the imperialists and reactionaries (again, their future is very bleak!). And revolutionary breakthroughs in various parts of the world will give great impetus and strength to the revolutionary minority everywhere, including in terms of influencing the (majority in the) middle.

The revolution is to a significant degree a civil war between two sections of the people (a point stressed in *Charting the Uncharted Course*).[25] This is certainly no less true or important in the U.S. than in other countries. By the time things reach the point of revolutionary warfare (versus counterrevolutionary warfare) we will have a significant base of support, and on the other side so will they — but, again, most of the people will be middle forces. Here stands out the importance of winning a significant number among these middle forces to "friendly neutrality." A big part of the timing of when to launch the armed struggle (or when to give spontaneous uprisings of masses the organized, all-around character of revolutionary warfare) is precisely concerned with finding the right circumstances to be able to win the greatest number of such middle forces to at least

[25] See *Charting The Uncharted Course*, from the Report of the 1980 Central Committee Meeting of the RCP,USA (Chicago: RCP Publications, 1981), p. 13 and following; see also Lenin, "Guerrilla Warfare," *LCW*, Vol. 11, pp. 213-233.

this "friendly neutrality," to have the other side (the imperialists and their reactionary social base) politically on the defensive and discredited among these middle forces to the greatest degree possible while our side and our forces have the initiative and political "credibility," especially among the advanced of the basic masses but also among the politically aware middle strata.

The Real Lessons of Grenada and Some Other Recent Events

Besides being yet another outrage committed by imperialism, the U.S. invasion and occupation of Grenada was a "cheap fix" for U.S. imperialism and its solid social base, which won't last long — and already isn't lasting against the strain of developing world events. That they needed something like *that* to get a "victory" and give a demonstration of "Resurgent America" (and get their social base salivating) certainly does not indicate strategic strength. Look, for example, at Lebanon and the problems they had there. It should be kept in mind that these problems were magnified in the short run by the fact that they aren't yet ready to (or at least haven't actually made the move to) get on with world war, but these problems are real enough in any case and more than that are a real indication of their strategic difficulties — something the advanced among the masses and the vanguard forces of the proletarian revolution should not lose sight of.

Vietnam was a powerful indication of the much more profound "flying apart" of their position and strength that could occur in the kind of world war they would have to engage in (including major nuclear exchanges, almost certainly). It is also possible that, if certain things come together, internationally and, as part of that, within the U.S., even further steps toward world war might give rise to serious conflict and crisis that could be seized on and turned into a revolutionary opportunity *if* the forces of the revolutionary proletariat are prepared and "tense."

We Are Just Waiting . . . But We're Not Just Waiting

We are just waiting for them to make a serious mistake — to take a serious fall and leave us a real opening. This is first of all a question of basic orientation and stand: it requires that radical rupture with reformism, with bourgeois democracy, and with patriotism; it requires the stand of *welcoming* such a disaster for "your own" ruling class.

We are "just waiting" for that — but on the other hand we are not just waiting: we are actively, urgently preparing. It is quite possible that they may not be able to withstand such a serious crisis, if . . . *if* we prepare and are "tense" in anticipation of just such an opening — which, it should be stressed, may come before world war is launched, exactly because of what the stakes are in such a war, what it will involve, and the widespread awareness of this among all different strata. Just the attempt to get "in position" from their side to launch such a war might create the openings in combination with the development of the overall world situation *and* our revolutionary work of preparation.

Ordinary People Rising to the Occasion

Here I am referring particularly to a situation — in a serious crisis, before or in the context of world war and/or a revolutionary civil war — where there may not be clear lines of leadership or organization within the party, or between the party and the masses; when the party's functioning may be disrupted, or perhaps the party is even (temporarily) shattered or wiped out in certain areas — precisely at a decisive time. In such extraordinary times there is all the more need for "ordinary people" — basic party members and basic masses trained in or even influenced in a general way by the party's line — to rise to the occasion and "take the reins and ride": regrouping revolutionary forces and rebuilding the party "from the ground up," taking initiative to give leadership and direction to the outrage and unrest of the masses and seeking out links with other forces of rebellion, while also striving to reestablish organizational links with the party structure in other areas. (Note in this regard some very relevant remarks by Mao: "When the war breaks out, it is best to rely on the local areas. You cannot depend on the central government."[26] He is speaking specifically of imperialist attacks on China and the likelihood of nuclear attacks as part of this.)

This is very much related to — and another dimension and graphic illustration of — the importance of political preparations *now*. In particular it dramatically illustrates the importance now of building the party at its base (among its main social base of proletarians without privilege and with really nothing but their chains to lose and a world to win) and of spreading and deepening the party's influence and roots among especially that base.

It is very important, as part of political (and ideological) preparation, to put some emphasis now on explaining this question of ordinary people rising to the occasion. The imperialists from their side are popularizing this kind of thing, reflecting their necessity given "what time it is" (here it is relevant to note what seems to be an increasing incidence of TV shows, etc., coming out in the U.S. now where ordinary housewives and others become CIA agents and so on!). We from our side and with directly opposite objectives and content to this must stress it all the more. An important part of this is popularizing historical examples of just this phenomenon of ordinary masses coming to the fore in extraordinary circumstances to take responsibility for the revolutionary movement and its vanguard forces, when this makes all the difference.

[26] Mao Tsetung, "Talk at Enlarged Meeting of the Political Bureau (March 20, 1966)," *Miscellany of Mao Tse-Tung Thought (1949-1968)* (Arlington, Virginia: Joint Publications Research Service, 1974), Part II, p. 378. Distributed by National Technical Information Service, U.S. Department of Commerce, Springfield, Va., 22151.

The Potential Role of Black (and Other) Prisoners

As a group, they can go either way; in fact they will split: there are some hard-core lumpen/criminal elements among them who will be much more likely to be in the counterrevolutionary camp when it comes down to it, but there are many who are much more victims than victimizers — victims of and opponents of this system. Many can play a very important role in the revolutionary camp when the time comes (and a number will make important contributions to the process of political preparation, as indeed more than a few already are, but this too will be magnified many times, in fact take on qualitatively new and different dimensions, when things reach the point of the armed struggle for power).

We would do great harm to the revolutionary cause — to the actual chances of winning — if we were not able to utilize, unleash, and channel this. Here, besides what is said on this in the *New Programme* of the party, Mao's comments on the use of similar forces, especially at the start of the revolutionary armed struggle in China, are worth thinking about: "When we started to fight battles, we depended on vagrants because they dared to die. There was a time when the army wanted to weed out the vagrant elements, but I opposed it."[27] On the other hand, he stressed from the beginning that the erroneous ideological and political tendencies that tend to arise among such forces, such as the "roving rebel band" mentality, must be firmly opposed, and that to be able to handle this it was crucial to strengthen the base of the party and the army among the basic working people — workers and peasants.[28] Yet, once again, Mao's policy was to find the ways to correct such mistaken tendencies and give

[27] Mao, "Highlights of Forum on Central Committee Work (December 20, 1964)," *Miscellany*, Part II, p. 421.

[28] See Mao, "On Correcting Mistaken Ideas in the Party," *MSW*, Vol. 1, pp. 105-116.

leadership to these forces and their positive qualitites — not to drive them out.

Their sights must be raised above the individual battle for survival (or individual dignity) and the individualist ideology that goes along with this — above, beyond the orientation of anything for such survival and dignity — which the material conditions of desperation (and still more of prison life) pull powerfully toward. It is the revolutionary ideology of the proletariat, and that ideology alone, which can so raise their sights and enable them to make a very valuable contribution to the revolutionary movement and, in particular, the armed struggle for power.

An Appeal to Those the System Has Cast Off

Here I am speaking not only to prisoners but to those whose life is lived on the desperate edge, whether or not they find some work; to those without work or even homes; to all those the system and its enforcers treat as so much human waste material.

Raise your sights above the degradation and madness, the muck and demoralization, above the individual battle to survive and to "be somebody" on the terms of the imperialists — of fouler, more monstrous criminals than mythology has ever invented or jails ever held. Become a part of the human saviors of humanity: the gravediggers of this system and the bearers of the future communist society.

This is not just talk or an attempt to make poetry here: there are great tasks to be fulfilled, great struggles to be carried out, and yes great sacrifices to be made to accomplish all this. But there is a world to save — and to win— and in that process those the system has counted as nothing can count for a great deal. They represent a great reserve force that must become an active force for the proletarian revolution, to destroy the old world and create the new.

QUESTIONS CONCERNING THE ACTUAL STRUGGLE FOR POWER

The Basic Context and the General Contours of the Armed Struggle to Overthrow U.S. Imperialism

As for our fundamental orientation, it is to do everything, during this stage of political preparation, to accelerate things toward the point where this armed struggle can be launched with a real prospect of keeping it going and fighting in such a way as to gather the strength to actually win; to do so before world war breaks out if there is any possibility of doing so in accordance with this perspective; and in any case, under whatever conditions, however horrendous — including in the course of such a world war or even in its aftermath — to continue working for and increasing our ability to seize the opportunities to shatter the power of imperialism (and all reaction) through revolutionary warfare. (Recalling here that apocalyptic statement in the 1979 forum speech on war — that even if only 500 people were left we would still have to wage and would wage class struggle and revolutionary war against would-be exploiters — this basic orientation is all the more important now, even more directly under the shadow of such a world war, and it must be understood even more fully in an *international* dimenson.) This, then, is our basic, general orientation.

In the present world context, the different general (and contradictory) possibilities, or eventualities, concerning revolutionary war and its relation to world war are:

(1) Revolution prevents world war, or world war is transformed into revolutionary war (even if in some aspects this bears a resemblance to the situation in the movie *Road Warrior*, with civil war between two sections of the survivors playing a significant part).

(2) With regard to each of the two above possibilities, there are in turn two possibilities, specifically in relation to (what is now) the U.S.: As for revolution preventing world war and specifically in terms of overthrowing U.S. imperialism, either a major impetus comes from revolutions in neighboring countries "spilling over" (minimally in terms of direct and immediate political influence) and sparking revolution in the U.S. itself; or the other way around, with the revolutionary struggle for power and revolutionary impetus coming first from within the U.S. itself and as it does so having great reverberations outward — indeed throughout the world as a whole but also very immediately and directly in neighboring countries. In all likelihood, things will go down through some combination of these two and with very powerful interaction between the revolutionary struggles. On the other hand, as for world war being transformed into revolutionary war, either this happens before massive destruction — meaning almost certainly nuclear devastation — or only afterward.

(3) A third "two possibilities" arises, which is very important to take into account in relation to revolutionary war and the establishment of a revolutionary regime in at least parts of the (former) U.S.: The possibility that the U.S. is hit with nuclear weapons as part of world war with the rival Soviet bloc (a very great possibility if such a war does break out), and/or the possibility that one or another group of imperialists uses nuclear weapons to attack the territory liberated through revolutionary war.

There are two main points to be emphasized in connection with all this:

(1) Much more emphasis must be given than has been up to now to the question of preventing world war — through revolution, which remains the only way to actually achieve such prevention as well as to eliminate the other crimes of this system. (Here some self-criticism must be made of our approach up to now, particularly the aspect of tending to view this world war as one that would drag out for quite awhile without a major qualitative leap in the destruction unleashed, that it would be a

protracted process of more or less gradually wearing out the opposing sides or "stretching them to the limit" — basically following the pattern of World War 1 or World War 2.)

(2) We must prepare for different possibilities and have the necessary flexibility to deal with these different eventualities — and many unforeseen and unforeseeable events, sudden and dramatic turns, leaps in the situation, and so on. And, even with certain necessary tactical shifts in our political work and overall revolutionary activity — such as the need for much more emphasis on actually preventing world war, through revolution — we must stick firmly to that fundamental orientation spoken to at the beginning of this section. All this must be the urgent concern of the revolutionaries and specifically the communist vanguard forces not just in particular countries but on the international level — and in this regard the formation and the *Declaration* of the Revolutionary Internationalist Movement represent a genuinely gigantic step, if only a beginning step.

Without a People's Army the People Have Nothing

When Mao made this statement (in 1945), he was summing up more than two decades of complex and rich experience in the Chinese Revolution, which almost from the beginning assumed the highest form of the revolutionary struggle — revolutionary warfare.[29] Already almost a decade earlier (in 1938, at the beginning of the anti-Japanese war), Mao stressed: "Without armed struggle the proletariat and the Communist Party would have no standing at all in China, and it would be impossible to accomplish any revolutionary task"[30] — impossible even to establish, or at least to maintain for long the anti-Japanese united front and War of Resistance. But he was also providing a succinct summary of a fundamental principle of revolution when he

[29] Mao, "On Coalition Government," *MSW*, Vol. 3, pp. 246-47.

[30] Mao, "Problems of War and Strategy," *MSW*, Vol. 2, p. 222. See also pp. 224-26.

said that "without a people's army the people have nothing."

In today's world situation there is a new and concentrated application of this principle. In a basic sense, during all wars the real deal, the real relations of power, are laid bare; as Lenin said, speaking specifically of war-induced crisis: "it is the great significance of all crises that they make manifest what has been hidden; they cast aside all that is relative, superficial, and trivial; they sweep away the political litter and reveal the real mainsprings of the *class struggle*."[31] A sharp expression of this is that wars — including revolutionary wars of course — make clear another basic truth formulated succinctly by Mao: "Political power grows out of the barrel of a gun."[32] But the approaching world-historic conjuncture, with its magnification of the prospects and effects of both war and revolution, will give a further, even a truly unprecedented expression to this basic truth.

This will certainly be so if revolution is able to prevent world war; and if it is not, then in the conditions of massive destruction — indeed the very likely shattering of the whole framework of human civilization as we now know it — there will be the fierce struggle to determine on what basis the reconstitution of some kind of society and the "starting up again" will be established. There can be no question that in such circumstances without revolutionary armed forces the revolutionary people will have nothing — because they (and you know whom I mean by "they") will still be around and still be determined, after all that, to reimpose their rule and their social relations. In this regard the presentation of "unrest" in *The Day After* is very striking. They shoot looters and (this is a fantasy on the imperialists' part) there's nobody around on the other side opposing this or doing anything with weapons to fight against and overthrow the remaining imperialist armed forces. It's just a few people looting and the state is there reimposing its order and there's the far-off voice of the President, giving political direction.

[31] Lenin, "Lessons of the Crisis," *LCW*, Vol. 24, p. 213.

[32] Mao, "Problems of War and Strategy," *MSW*, Vol. 2, p. 224.

But again, even in a distorted (and fantasized!) form, this is a sharp illustration of the point: without a people's army the people have nothing.

Involved in all this is the crucial question of the relationship between the proletarian party and the revolutionary army (or in more general terms, between the overall political leadership of the revolution and the armed forces of the revolution). At the very same time that he summarized the basic truth that all political power grows out of the barrel of a gun, Mao also insisted on a no less decisive principle: "the Party commands the gun, and the gun must never be allowed to command the Party."[33] The importance of this is underscored by the fact that, while the most reliable base for the party, on which it must base its strength and where its roots must be deeply established, is the revolutionary proletariat, and while in an overall sense this must also be the main basis for the revolutionary army led by the party, on the other hand (as spoken to earlier) it will be necessary to bring into that army, from its very founding, many youth and others who do not have the experience nor the fully developed outlook or discipline characteristic of the class-conscious proletariat. Mao's comments on "vagrants" and what he called "brave elements" are very much to the point here; and it is very unlikely that a revolutionary army could be built or a revolutionary war won without the vigorous participation of a good number of such elements. The refusal to involve them could only be an expression of conservatism and ultimately of pessimism and defeatism.

On the other hand, this gives all the more emphasis not only to the principle that the party must give leadership to and develop the proletarian class consciousness and discipline of these elements — and that in an overall and all-around sense the party must command the gun and not the other way around — but also to the fact that in party-building and in army-building (when that is the order of the day), the bedrock basis must be

[33] Mao, "Problems of War and Strategy," *MSW*, Vol. 2, p. 224.

class-conscious proletarians. For in a fundamental sense, as Lenin put it, "Only the proletariat can create the nucleus of a mighty revolutionary army, mighty both in its ideals, its discipline, its organization, and its heroism in the struggle."[34]

Returning to the Border Question

In the article "The Border Question" (in *Reflections and Sketches*) I expressed my strong conviction that the revolution in (what is now) the U.S. must not only be internationa*list* in its character and guiding ideology but to a significant degree will of necessity also be internationa*l*, and that it will not be possible to succeed in this revolution without educating the masses in the understanding and spirit that there is nothing whatsoever sacred (or worth defending as such) about the present borders of the U.S., which have been established anyway on the basis of plunder, pillage, and literal genocide.[35] This fundamental point of strategic orientation is heightened by the points I have stressed on the consequences of world war (the destructiveness of the nuclear exchanges that would almost certainly be involved and the "fallout" from this in the broadest, fullest sense). But, on the other hand, in terms of the possibility of preventing world war through revolution — and certainly revolution in the U.S. would be a gigantic factor in that — this revolution certainly will not be successful by seeking to confine itself to the present boundaries of the U.S.

It is hardly conceivable that there could be a revolution in the U.S. which didn't at some point and in various ways significantly interpenetrate with and have mutual interaction and mutual influence with revolutionary struggles being waged by the people in the neighboring countries — especially in Cen-

[34] Lenin, "Between Two Battles," *LCW*, Vol. 9, p. 465.

[35] "The Border Question," *RW*, No. 174 (October 1, 1983), p. 3.

tral America. And without falling into "Lin Biaoism,"[36] it is correct, from a strategic, overall point of view, to be aware of the ways in which these neighboring oppressed nations have particular aspects of a "countryside" in relation to the revolution in the U.S. "city" — though, unlike "Lin Biaoism" that does not mean sitting around waiting for revolutionary struggles there to "ripen" the revolutionary situation in the U.S. It does mean accelerating and intensifying the work of preparation for revolution right in the U.S. itself.

In "Crowns Will Roll By Dozens on the Pavements . . ." I stressed that a third world war would "batter down the barriers of country and nation much more than any previous war," while

> at the same time it will destroy more than ever before the superstitious awe for states and statecraft that is instilled in the masses, will make clear that boundaries and governments are established and enforced with cannon and missile and there is nothing holy or eternal about them, or about the ruling classes presently presiding over the fate of mankind with such unspeakable consequences for it.[37]

In striving to make revolution in the U.S., including before the outbreak of world war and as a perhaps decisive factor in preventing that war, we should keep firmly in mind and base ourselves on this same fundamental understanding and orientation.

[36] Here I am referring specifically to the theory that revolutions in the Third World would "surround" and eventually destroy imperialism — U.S. imperialism in particular. This theory went beyond the correct recognition that since World War 2 the Third World has been the most fertile area for revolutionary struggle and in the period of the 1960s in particular was a storm center of revolution. It basically wrote off the possibility of revolution in the imperialist citadels themselves, essentially seeing the destruction of imperialism — again, U.S. imperialism in particular — coming solely from outside, from the encircling and tightening stranglehold of revolution in the Third World. This theory was especially prominent in the 1960s and was particularly associated with Lin Biao, a top leader of the Chinese Communist Party and Defense Minister of the People's Republic of China until he met his death after an unsuccessful attempt to overthrow the leadership of Mao Tsetung (even plotting to assassinate Mao) and carry out a pro-Soviet revisionist coup in 1971.

[37] "Crowns Will Roll By Dozens on the Pavements . . . There Will Be Nobody There to Pick Them Up," *RW*, No. 115 (September 31, 1981), p. 3.

Making Good on the Task Set Forth in *Coming From Behind to Make Revolution*

In *Coming From Behind to Make Revolution* I discussed the fact that, in the realm of military science, military theory, and strategic thinking, "we are behind the bourgeoisie" and that here too was a sphere where we must make systematic efforts to overcome this gap. At the same time I stressed that this is not a mystery that cannot be mastered but "it is a science,. . .it is a serious question that must and can be taken up and conquered" with the guidance of Marxism-Leninism-Mao Tsetung Thought and learning from historical experience, especially the historical experience of the revolutionary proletariat in this sphere. Further, I stressed with regard to the military tasks in a country like the U.S. that it is also a question of "charting an uncharted course": such a successful revolutionary war has not yet been waged by the proletariat in an advanced imperialist country.[38] In this we can take guidance and inspiration from Mao who noted that "the phenomenon of war is more elusive and is characterized by greater uncertainty than any other social phenomenon, in other words. . .it is more a matter of 'probability.' Yet war is in no way supernatural, but a mundane process governed by necessity."[39] And especially with what is on the historical agenda and the stakes involved, we have work to do to make good on the task set forth in *Coming From Behind* and to begin to conquer this sphere — first in the realm of theory as essential preparation for conquering in practical, literally life-and-death struggle.

It is true and a fundamental point of orientation that only so much can be accomplished by studying military theory. As Mao put it: "Reading is learning, but applying is also learning and the more important kind of learning at that. Our chief method is to

[38] Bob Avakian, *Coming From Behind to Make Revolution and Crucial Questions in Coming From Behind* (Chicago: RCP Publications, 1980), p. 18.

[39] Mao, "On Protracted War," *MSW*, Vol. 2, p. 164.

learn warfare through warfare."[40] But, on the other hand, to raise this as a reason not to take up serious and systematic study in this sphere, even at a time when the conditions do not yet exist in the U.S. for applying them directly (for actually waging revolutionary war), is to ignore the fact that learning through study, if not the chief method of learning overall, is still a very important method. Further, to oppose such study is to work against waging the revolutionary war on the most correct and effective basis when it is time. In short, without such study "in advance" the preparation for revolution is not thorough, and at the outbreak of the revolutionary crisis and actual armed struggle — spontaneous armed struggle and/or armed struggle organized by revolutionary forces — revolutionary forces will not be where they could be at such a crucial point. This is one important aspect, in the theoretical sphere, of the point stressed by the *Declaration* of the Revolutionary Internationalist Movement: "Even when conditions do not yet exist for the armed struggle of the masses, communists must carry out the necessary work in preparation for the emergence of such conditions."[41]

Some Differences Between the Bolshevik and the Chinese Army-Building Experiences, and Some Lessons From This

An essential difference is that the character of the Chinese Revolution was such that (as noted earlier) almost from the beginning and more or less continuously for over two decades the revolutionary struggle assumed its highest form of armed struggle. At first the Communist Party was in a united front — in fact was in the same umbrella-type organization, the Kuomintang (KMT) — with bourgeois political forces. This opened up

[40] Mao, "Problems Of Strategy In China's Revolutionary War," *MSW*, Vol. 1, pp. 189-90.

[41] *Declaration of the Revolutionary Internationalist Movement*, p. 29.

possibilities for study and training (in military academies and other ways) under conditions less repressive than would otherwise have obtained. The lack of a strong unified government also made it possible, even before the Communist Party formed its own independent armed forces, to accumulate experience in warfare alongside (or, again, within the same broad organizational structure as) bourgeois military forces.[42] Thus, when the KMT was seized by Chiang Kai-shek and turned into a counter-revolutionary instrument, thus beginning the first civil war in China between the KMT and the Communist Party, the latter had already accumulated valuable experience in warfare and developed the basis and core of leadership for forming its own independent armed forces. From there, through several different phases of the struggle, and many twists and turns, they built up, over two decades of warfare, a military force powerful enough to finally win nationwide political power, including a tested and tempered leadership cadre, as well as basic military doctrine and principles of operation, strategy, and tactics — all concentrated in the military line of Mao Tsetung.

In contrast, the Bolsheviks had to "telescope" all this. They had some limited experience in the unsuccessful 1905 Revolution but basically had to "start from scratch" in the urgent, acute circumstances of the October 1917 insurrection and the civil war that followed. Right after consolidating the power won through the October Revolution and its immediate momentum, they had to demobilize the old army and then begin right away to build up a new Red Army "all at once." (The fact that the peasants-in-uniform in the old army were unwilling to continue fighting in the immediate aftermath of October was one of the main reasons the new Bolshevik government had to sign the Brest-Litovsk Treaty, making major concessions to the German imperialists.)

But in building up the new revolutionary army they utilized

[42] See, for example, Mao, "Why Is It That Red Political Power Can Exist in China?", *MSW*, Vol. 1, p. 66.

to a considerable degree the old structure and the old officers and specialists of the former Tsarist armed forces while raising new officers from the ranks and politically "surrounding" the old officers with communist commissars. And to a significant degree they based themselves on the military doctrine of the old armed forces.[43]

Lenin was quite frank in stating, right in the midst of the civil war of 1918-1920, that "the organization of a Red Army was an entirely new question which had never been dealt with before, even theoretically."[44] And he put the problem this way:

> How was a class which had hitherto served as cannon-fodder for the military commanders of the ruling imperialist class to create its own commanders? How was it to solve the problem of combining the enthusiasm, the new revolutionary creative spirit of the oppressed and the employment of the store of the bourgeois science and technology of militarism in their worst forms without which this class would not be able to master modern technology and modern methods of warfare?[45]

The approach the Bolsheviks took to resolving this contradiction was, as noted, to make use of the old officers and specialists, and to a significant degree the old military doctrine in which these officers and specialists were expert, while politically "surrounding" these officers and specialists with communist

[43] In this regard, it is very interesting to note that Lenin had argued, during the course of the 1905 Revolution — which ended in defeat, it is important to remember here — that "military science has proved that a people's militia is quite practicable, that it can rise to the military tasks presented by a war both of defense and of attack" (Lenin, "The Armed Forces and the Revolution," *LCW*, Vol. 10, pp. 56-57). And this was urged directly in opposition to the need for a standing army, since,Lenin argued, "The experience of Western Europe has shown how utterly reactionary the standing army is" (Vol. 10, p. 56). But the experience of the successful revolution in Russia in 1917 and its aftermath, as well as the experience of proletarian revolution since then, has shown that a militia has not been adequate and it is necessary to build up a new, revolutionary standing army.

[44] Lenin, "The Eighth Congress of the R.C.P.(B.) (March 18- 23, 1919)," *LCW*, Vol. 29, p. 152.

[45] Lenin, "The Eighth Congress of the R.C.P.(B.)," *LCW*, Vol. 29, p. 153.

commissars (and raising new officers and specialists from the ranks). Lenin argued bluntly that the victories of the Red Army in the civil war would not have been possible without utilizing these old officers and specialists. He even stated flatly that "there are tens of thousands of old colonels and officers of other ranks in that [Red] army and if we had not accepted them in our service and made them serve us, we could not have created an army."[46]

The experience of the Chinese Revolution was much richer in regard to revolutionary warfare and the approach to military doctrine, to the question of developing a revolutionary army with revolutionary politics in command, of the relation between weapons, overall technology, and expertise on the one hand, and what Mao called "the conscious, dynamic role of man" on the other — all this, in terms of basic approach, is much more of a "model" for the revolutionary proletariat, not just in Third World countries, but in general, even though in many situations, including that of our party in the U.S., there will be aspects of "telescoping" similar to the experience of the Bolsheviks. Still, this has not of course solved all the problems the international proletariat will encounter in waging revolutionary warfare, nor did it completely solve the problem of the standing army tending to become an instrument in the hands of revisionists.[47]

[46] Lenin, "A Speech Delivered at the First All-Russia Conference on Party Work in the Countryside (November 18, 1919)," *LCW*, Vol. 30, p. 147. To a large degree, this approach was forced on the Bolsheviks. It was a matter of pressing necessity and the imminent danger of defeat combined with the fact that, as Lenin frankly stated, this was an entirely new problem for the proletariat. But, unfortunately, the basic military structure and much of the same military doctrine remained unchanged and was perpetuated in the Soviet Red Army. This was one of the significant factors contributing to the sharply contradictory experience of the Soviet Union in World War 2, when bourgeois tendencies in Soviet society "flowered" and this assumed concentrated expression in the armed forces, so that the war was won but at great cost, politically, to the proletariat, leaving its rule of society precarious and highly vulnerable to counter-revolution from within — a point I addressed in *Conquer the World* (see especially pp. 21-28).

[47] It is worth recalling that one of the main phenomena, one of the main dangers, pointed to by Mao and his followers in their last great, and unfortunately unsuccessful, battle, was the large number of veteran military leaders who had turned revisionist and turned the People's Liberation Army into an instrument of the new bourgeoisie in the Party itself — those old veterans who crossed snow-capped mountains on the Long March and still wear red stars on their army caps but are some of the biggest cases of bourgeois democrats turning into capitalist-roaders.

Most fundamentally, just seeking to mechanically apply or "rest with" the military doctrine and principles developed through the course of the Chinese Revolution — concentrated in Mao's military line — won't do, it won't be sufficient to guide revolutionary armed struggle to victory, as much as this line does in fact represent a genuinely immortal contribution to the proletarian revolution and its scientific theory. This is because, as Mao himself insisted, revolution (and all life) is not a stagnant pond but an ever-rushing great river; and more specifically (as Mao himself also repeatedly stressed) war is one of the spheres where one finds most powerfully expressed the basic truth that no great event appears in the same form, in all significant aspects, as similar great events before it; where fluidity, change, and surprise are most essential features; and where the need to act in accordance with all this is most prominently expressed.

In War as in Revolution: The Next Time Is not the Same as the Last

It is a general principle (or truth) in war, noted and stressed by even bourgeois military "experts" (at least the really knowledgeable and insightful ones), that every war (or at least every major one) is different in many important aspects from the previous ones. (Some examples of this: World War 2 as compared with World War 1, including not only such tactics as the "blitzkrieg" employed by the Germans but generally the much more fluid and mobile character of the ground fighting, the different and more prominent role of naval warfare as well as its combination with air power, which itself was a far greater factor throughout, even before the use of that completely new type of weapon at the end of the war: the atomic bomb! Other examples are Korea, and much more dramatically Vietnam, as compared with World War 2, for U.S. imperialism in particular.) It is also generally something that many insightful bourgeois experts comment on — and wring their hands over — that after a major war there is a strong tendency, especially among the victorious forces, to carry on afterward with the same military doctrine and even the same specific tactical orientation as was developed and applied in that war: to settle into the rut of routine and be carried along by habit and inertia. (And I think that tendencies of this kind are bound to exert a strong pull on any military power, and all the more so the more it is burdened with a massive and top-heavy apparatus and command structure.)

This is a problem for us (the international proletariat) too, especially where we win state power and of necessity develop our own standing armies but also more generally in the handling of the contradiction of learning from historical experience, especially the experience of revolutionary war and most especially revolutionary war waged by the proletariat, while on the other hand applying this concretely to the new and different conditions we will inevitably face. This is linked with the principle that revolution — and this is certainly no less true of proletarian revolution than other, previous revolutions in history — can only be made by breaking with certain established, perhaps even somewhat codified, "norms," precepts, and practices. This is a point I stressed in *Mao Tsetung's Immortal Contributions*[48] and again in *For a Harvest of Dragons*. But in the latter work in particular I also stressed that the development of revolutionary theory and strategic thinking, necessarily involving ruptures with some aspects of the previously accepted theory and practice, must be done and can only be done correctly on the basis of upholding and building from — while making leaps from — the basic principles of Marxism as they have been developed up to the given time.[49]

It is with this foundation that the necessary and crucial initiative must be taken and innovations made. It is not at all sur-

[48] Bob Avakian, *Mao Tsetung's Immortal Contributions* (Chicago: RCP Publications, 1979), especially Chapter 7: "Mao Tsetung, the Greatest Revolutionary of Our Time," pp. 311-24.

[49] Bob Avakian, *For a Harvest of Dragons: On the "Crisis of Marxism" and the Power of Marxism — Now More Than Ever* (Chicago: RCP Publications, 1983), especially Chapter 2: "Marxism in its Development into Marxism-Leninism, Mao Tsetung Thought," pp. 57-114.

prising, then, that this should be of great significance in revolutionary warfare, since as Mao formulated it:

> The seizure of power by armed force, the settlement of the issue by war, is the central task and the highest form of revolution. This Marxist-Leninist principle of revolution holds good universally, for China and for all other countries.
>
> But while the principle remains the same, its application by the party of the proletariat finds expression in varying ways according to the varying conditions.[50]

The principle that the next war will differ in important aspects from the last one will find much more concentrated and dramatic expression than ever before in the approaching world-historic conjuncture, on both the side of the proletariat and revolutionary people and that of the imperialists and reactionaries. A particularly important aspect of this, and a peculiar feature of the approaching conjuncture, is that the explosion of the major world contradictions — even if world war is prevented by revolution — will almost certainly witness the extremes of advanced technological methods of warfare on the one hand and "primitive" methods of warfare on the other. As one example, look at the youth in the video arcades that have sprung up everywhere, playing all the war-game machines, as well as others. The imperialists, of course, are actively promoting this, but it is far from determined on which side and for which cause these youth will ultimately use such acquired skills — strategically the interests of the majority of youth lie with revolution and fighting with the revolutionary armed forces against imperialism and reaction. So on the one hand many youth, including those won to the revolutionary side, will be utilizing such skills while, especially on the side of the revolutionary forces, it will be

[50] Mao, "Problems of War and Strategy," *MSW*, Vol. 2, p. 219. Lenin also argued that "war is not only a continuation of politics, it is the epitome of politics" (Lenin, "Seventh All-Russia Congress of Soviets," *LCW*, Vol. 30, p. 224) — a point that must be returned to and discussed in various aspects.

necessary to engage in literal street fighting and other forms of basic warfare that involve "low-technology" weapons and methods.

Especially given all this, as a basic point of orientation we must be prepared to go thoroughly into and conquer, in theory and practice, this terrain — of warfare and revolutionary warfare in particular — in the face of truly unprecedented conditions. In this light we must take in deeply Mao's summation that "all who take part in war must rid themselves of their customary ways and accustom themselves to war before they can win victory."[51] At the same time, we will have to learn how to do this without "losing ourselves" in war and losing sight of our larger goals and indeed the whole purpose and orientation with which communists take up the task of waging revolutionary war. For as Mao also stressed:

> Some people ridicule us as advocates of the "omnipotence of war." Yes, we are advocates of the omnipotence of revolutionary war; that is good, not bad, it is Marxist. . . . We are advocates of the abolition of war, we do not want war; but war can only be abolished through war, and in order to get rid of the gun it is necessary to take up the gun.[52]
>
> When human society advances to the point where classes and states are eliminated, there will be no more wars, counterrevolutionary or revolutionary, unjust or just; that will be the era of perpetual peace for mankind. Our study of the laws of revolutionary war springs from the desire to eliminate all wars; herein lies the distinction between us Communists and all the exploiting classes.[53]

In other words, the ultimate objective with which communists wage the revolutionary armed struggle — to achieve classless society, communism — means and is inseparable from the elimination of the basis or need for war of any kind; this is true of the

[51] Mao, "On Protracted War," *MSW*, Vol. 2, p. 154.

[52] Mao. "Problems of War and Strategy," *MSW*, Vol. 2, p. 225.

[53] Mao, "Problems of Strategy in China's Revolutionary War," *MSW*, Vol. 1, p. 183.

proletariat and its communist vanguard and of no other class or social force. And, as I put it in the conclusion of *For a Harvest of Dragons*:

> One of the significant if perhaps subtle and often little-noticed ways in which the enemy, even in defeat, seeks to exact revenge on the revolution and sow the seed of its future undoing is in what he would force the revolutionaries to become in order to defeat him. It will come to this: we will have to face him in the trenches and defeat him amidst terrible destruction but we must not in the process annihilate the fundamental difference between the enemy and ourselves. Here the example of Marx is illuminating: he repeatedly fought at close quarters with the ideologists and apologists of the bourgeoisie but he never fought them on their terms or with their outlook; with Marx his method is as exhilarating as his goal is inspiring. We must be able to maintain our firmness of principles but at the same time our flexibility, our materialism and our dialectics, our realism and our romanticism, our solemn sense of purpose and our sense of humor.[54]

"You Fight Your Way and I'll Fight My Way"

Mao says at one point that all military logic, whatever the particulars, can be reduced to this.[55] This does not supersede (and he does not argue that it supersedes) what he describes as the basic principle or object of warfare: to preserve oneself and destroy the enemy, in which the second aspect is principal and decisive.[56] Mao's point is that "You fight your way and I'll fight my way" is the basic doctrine or strategic orientation for applying this basic principle, for achieving this basic object of warfare.

[54] Avakian, *For a Harvest of Dragons*, p. 152.

[55] See Mao, "You Fight Your Way and I'll Fight My Way — A Conversation With Palestine Liberation Organization (March 1965)," *Miscellany*, Part II, pp. 447-48.

[56] See, for example, Mao, "On Protracted War," *MSW*, Vol. 2, p. 156.

One specific elaboration of this by Mao — "if I can win, I will fight; if I cannot win, I will run away"[57] — may not be strictly applicable in all situations, particularly the "run away" aspect, since it relies on being in a situation affording the ability to maneuver and avoid battle (maneuver in time as well as in space). But in an overall sense and as a basic orientation this formulation — "You fight your way and I'll fight my way" — applies and is of great importance, specifically to the strategic orientation of not *initiating* battle unless conditions are favorable.

With regard to the imperialists and reactionaries generally, if they can't fight their way — as they are deprived of the ability to fight their way — their strategic weaknesses will increasingly show up; and so it must be a major objective of the revolutionary army precisely to deprive them of that ability. Particularly up against a revolutionary army, they depend on utilizing, and intimidating and overpowering the other side with, superior technology and (at the start) superior numbers. They depend especially on extensive air power not only for heavy bombardment but also to amass combat force and for mobility generally. In this regard it is interesting to note a telling comment in one of the numerous "my true story as a soldier in Vietnam" novels in recent years: Frederick Downs, the author of this one, *The Killing Zone*, says perhaps more than he meant to when he writes, "The noisy fuss of a helicopter was always welcome, dustoff or not. It reassured us of the tremendous system backing us up."[58] Imperialist and reactionary troops generally cannot fight effectively, or sustain effective fighting, without such "reassurance," especially when they are up against revolutionary armed forces representing and fighting for the interests of the masses of people.

Again, when imperialist and reactionary armies are deprived of the ability to fight their way — to overwhelm and pound the enemy with superior technology and force — then their strategic weaknesses increasingly stand out: they are an

[57] Mao, "You Fight Your Way and I'll Fight My Way," *Miscellany*, Part II, p. 447.

[58] Frederick Downs, *The Killing Zone* (New York: Berkley Books, 1983), p. 144.

army of plunder and exploitation, opposed to the interests of the masses of people worldwide; their troops have no real political consciousness or awareness of the actual interests and objectives they are fighting for; they rely on technology and technological superiority and therefore are at a loss to a great degree when they do not have it or it is effectively neutralized; their ranks are organized in a strict, oppressive hierarchy and command structure and are riddled with acute class and national (and male/female) contradictions and conflicts, including among the "grunts" themselves as well as between officers and rank-and-file soldiers. And all this will gather momentum once it has begun to strongly assert its influence.

All this is also an expression of another basic principle formulated and fought fiercely for by Mao: people, not weapons, are decisive in warfare.[59] In a fundamental sense, an army is a concentration of the society it is fighting for — of the social and political relations, values, etc., that are dominant and characterize that society (recall here the statement by Lenin cited earlier that war is not only the continuation but the epitome of politics); and the fundamental difference between revolutionary armies and counterrevolutionary armies will continue to find fuller expression the more a war between them goes on. This is one of the most significant aspects of the importance of being able to keep the revolutionary war going and gathering momentum once it has been initiated.

To get to the point where this is possible — to initiate the armed struggle and be able to continue it to the point of being able (to at least begin) to deprive the imperialists and reactionaries of the ability to fight their way depends on the development of the objective world situation, but a very important part of that is revolutionary struggle and mass protest and rebellion not only in the U.S. but worldwide. And even favorable developments in the objective situation which might provide revolutionary opportunities will be lost without the orientation and the po-

[59] See, for example, Mao, "On Protracted War," *MSW*, Vol. 2, p. 143.

litical "tenseness" to be able to recognize and seize the moment to go over to insurrectionary struggle. This is another expression of the importance of political preparation of the masses, especially of the advanced, as well as of the party itself, from now looking forward to the time when the insurrection can be launched and coordinated into revolutionary war for political power.

From the beginning the insurrection must be viewed not as a thing unto itself but as the beginning of a civil war (even if there should be a brief interval before all-out civil war, as occurred in Russia after October 1917). As Lenin summed up in the midst of the civil war in Russia:

> Never in history has there been a revolution in which it was possible to lay down one's arms and rest on one's laurels after the victory. . . .
>
> Revolutions are subjected to the most serious tests in the fire of battle. If you are oppressed and exploited and think of throwing off the power of the exploiters, if you are determined to carry this to its logical conclusion, you must understand that you will have to contend against the onslaught of the exploiters of the whole world. If you are ready to offer resistance and to make further sacrifices in order to hold out in the struggle, you are a revolutionary; if not, you will be crushed.[60]

Thus the insurrection and civil war to follow must be viewed, strategically, as a whole, and in an overall sense must be guided by a unified doctrine and strategic orientation.

This is especially important given the concrete conditions and relations in the U.S., where the social base for proletarian revolution is concentrated so preponderantly in the "urban cores" and where a key question from the beginning of the armed insurrection will be to "break out" of an enemy encirclement, containment, and suppression of these "cores." In fact, the emergence of a situation in which there is a "good shot" at doing this in at least a number of major urban concentrations is a decisive aspect of the objective conditions needed to launch the armed struggle for power.

[60] Lenin, "The Achievements and Difficulties of the Soviet Government," *LCW*, Vol. 29, pp. 67-68.

Offense and Defense

The offensive is decisive — and the defensive is death — in insurrection; the objective of this insurrection is at least to establish some kind of revolutionary regime, encompassing as much territory and as many people as possible but viable enough to act as a relatively secure rear for the revolutionary armed forces in the civil war.

First, on the offensive in insurrection. On the eve of the October 1917 Revolution, in refuting those who argued that an insurrection could not succeed and if it did the Bolsheviks could not retain state power anyway, Lenin quoted Marx at length on the "art of insurrection," and it is worth repeating here much of what Lenin quoted:

> Firstly, never play with insurrection unless you are fully prepared to go the whole way. . . . "Insurrection is an equation with very indefinite magnitudes, the value of which may change every day; the forces opposed to you have all the advantage of organization, discipline and habitual authority. . .; unless you bring strong odds against them you are defeated and ruined. Secondly, once you have entered upon the insurrectionary career, act with the greatest determination, and on the offensive. The defensive is the death of every armed rising; it is lost before it measures itself with its enemies. Surprise your antagonists while their forces are scattered, prepare the way for new successes, however small, but prepare daily; keep up the moral superiority which the first successful rising has given to you; rally in this way those vacillating elements to your side which always follow the strongest impulse and which always look out for the safer side; force your enemies to retreat before they can collect their strength against you. . . ."[61]

[61] See Lenin, "Can the Bolsheviks Retain State Power?", *LCW*, Vol. 26, p. 132; see also Lenin, "Advice of an Onlooker," *LCW*, Vol. 26, p. 180. It is significant that, already in the 1905 Revolution, which proved unsuccessful, those who were to lead the successful revolution of October 1917 and following, in particular Lenin and Stalin as well, began to focus on these crucial points. See for example Stalin's citation of similar

Lenin had also summed up from the experience of 1905 that "every beginning is difficult, as the saying goes. It was very difficult for the workers to go over to the armed combat . . ."; and this gives all the more emphasis to the fact that there must be no wavering, no "playing at insurrection" once it has been decided on. This is why Lenin later (on the eve of the October 1917 Revolution) tore into those pseudorevolutionaries who "'conveniently' forget, of course, that a firm party line, its unyielding resolve, is *also* a mood-creating *factor*, particularly at the sharpest revolutionary moments."[62] It is also why, at the same crucial hour, Lenin even went so far as to say, "The seizure of power is the business of the uprising; its political purpose will become clear after the seizure."[63]

On the other hand, Lenin not only consistently fought for the position that throughout the political preparation for the eventual insurrection the masses must be enabled to consciously grasp the aims and methods of the revolutionary struggle, but even during the 1905 Revolution he had stressed that the establishment of a revolutionary government, "if only at first in a small part of the country," was a necessary and crucial step, among other things, to "give full scope to the revolutionary creative activity of the masses, who participate but little in this activity in time of peace, but who come to the forefront in revolutionary epochs."[64] Overall, Lenin summed up then, "a revolutionary government is as vitally essential at the present stage of the popular

---

observations by Engels in Stalin's summation of especially the experience of the Moscow uprising of 1905. Among other things, Engels says that even an uprising "begun in a brainless way" could have a chance of leading to success if it is quickly and resolutely followed up on and its momentum built off of to sweep across as much of the country as possible, drawing in more and more forces, winning over wavering elements, and deepening splits and causing desertions among the enemy armed forces. Food for thought! And this, by the way, is another reason why armed struggle can accomplish what elections never can in activating masses and winning over even waverers in the struggle to upend and uproot the old order (see J.V. Stalin, "Marx and Engels on Insurrection," *Works* [Moscow: Progress Publishers, 1954], Vol. 1, p. 247).

[62] Lenin, "Letter to Comrades," *LCW*, Vol. 26, p. 209.

[63] Lenin, "Letter to Central Committee Members," *LCW*, Vol. 26, p. 235.

[64] Lenin, "The Revolutionary Army and the Revolutionary Government," *LCW*, Vol. 8, p. 563.

uprising [i.e., its initial stage — *B.A.*] as a revolutionary army.... The revolutionary government is necessary for the political unification and the political organization of the insurgent section of the people."[65] This sheds further light on the fact that the objective of the insurrection must be, while seeking to conquer as much as can be in the initial stage, to minimally establish a revolutionary regime, if only at first in a part of the country, to act as a relatively secure base area (rear) for the revolutionary armed forces.

There will be, of course, important differences between the process of revolutionary warfare in different countries and in particular between the two basic types of countries — imperialist states and oppressed nations — and in the latter it will be the general rule that forms of guerrilla warfare in particular areas, rather than simultaneous insurrectionary uprisings, will characterize the first stages of the revolutionary war. But in these cases too the objective is to establish revolutionary base areas, embryonic revolutionary regimes, as a rear for carrying forward the revolutionary war. (In this connection, in discussing the basis for protracted war in China, at that point against Japan, Mao argues the following: "The heterogeneity and uneven development of China's economy are rather advantageous in the war of resistance." He adds the observation, very provocative to ponder in terms of revolutionary warfare in the advanced imperialist countries: "to sever Shanghai from the rest of China would definitely not be as disastrous to China as would be the severance of New York from the rest of the United States.")[66]

From the beginning of the insurrection there will be what Lenin called the *"fight for the troops."*[67] But, as he insisted, the launching of the insurrection does not depend on nor can it wait for the winning over of the troops of the reactionary army. It will precisely be a fight between the revolutionary and the counter-

[65] Lenin, "The Revolutionary Army and the Revolutionary Government," *LCW*, Vol. 8, p. 563.

[66] Mao Tsetung, "On Protracted War," *MSW*, Vol. 2, p. 118.

[67] See Lenin, "Lessons of the Moscow Uprising," *LCW*, Vol. 11, p. 174.

revolutionary camps for the allegiance of the rank-and-file troops of the reactionary army, and precisely the winning of these troops (or many of them, since it would be foolish to expect to win them all) depends on the initiation of the armed insurrection when the time is ripe, and then on the daring and determination of the insurrectionaries, the increasing polarization of the situation and especially the momentum gained by the insurrection as it advances quickly upon each victory and from each position conquered.

It is this that Lenin is speaking to when he notes that the uprising in Moscow in December 1905 "strikingly confirmed one of Marx's profound propositions: revolution progresses by giving rise to a strong and united counterrevolution, i.e., it compels the enemy to resort to more and more extreme measures of defense and in this way devises ever more powerful means of attack."[68] There is no way to get around the fact that it is necessary to *defeat*, militarily, the armed forces of counterrevolution on the battlefield — "we shall prove to be miserable pedants if we forget that at a time of uprising there must also be a physical struggle for the troops," Lenin remarked.[69] An insurrection should not be launched without a perspective for doing just that, and for handling to advantage the dialectic Lenin (citing Marx) refers to just above (revolutionary armed struggle compels the counterrevolution to adopt more and more extreme measures of defense, requiring in turn even more powerful means of attack). Winning over significant sections of the troops of the counterrevolutionary armed forces depends on demoralizing them, which in turn depends on defeating them in battle and putting them into disarray.

All this is linked to the often-asked question: where do the revolutionary armed forces get their weapons from, especially at the start? The answer provided by historical experience and revolutionary principles summed up from it is that, overwhelm-

[68] Lenin, "Lessons of the Moscow Uprising," *LCW*, Vol. 11, p. 172.

[69] Lenin, "Lessons of the Moscow Uprising," *LCW*, Vol. 11, pp. 174-75.

ingly, especially at the start, the weapons of the revolutionary armed forces come from the enemy — that is, they are captured; and the capturing of these weapons is one of the most important objects of the revolutionary army in waging battles.

Mao described how, even after nearly two decades of waging war, the Chinese revolutionary army still faced the situation, at the start of the second (and final) civil war with the KMT, where

> we did not have any large cities. We did not have the assistance of foreign powers, our troops were few in numbers [i.e., relative to those of the KMT — *B.A.*], we had no air force, we had no navy, we had no airplanes, and we had no artillery. We only had light weapons. They were not made by us; they had been seized by us.[70]

Here it is important to note not just that to a large degree the weapons they had were ones they seized from the KMT (Mao also referred to the U.S. as the "quartermaster" of the Chinese People's Liberation Army because it funneled so many weapons and other materiel to the PLA through the KMT, which the U.S. was massively supplying) but also that in effect they took only what they could use — to wage *revolutionary warfare.* They did not attempt to take (but sought to destroy) what was not of advantage in waging such a war (this is another important dimension to Mao's statement of what they did *not* have and the fact that all they had, at the start, were light weapons). This, however, is not some kind of absolute injunction against the use of modern weaponry; rather it is an expression of the fact that weapons are secondary and their use (and usefulness, or lack of it) is determined at any point by what kind of war is being fought and what — or who — is being relied on as the main factor.

Returning to the relation of offense and defense, it is important to grasp that this is a dialectical relationship — they are a unity of opposites, and as such they interpenetrate back and

[70] Mao, "Conversation with Zanzibar Expert M.M. Ali and his Wife (June 18, 1964)," *Miscellany*, Part II, p. 369.

forth in the course of war, of major campaigns, and of battles (defense within offense and vice versa). One of the more important and insightful discussions in Clausewitz's military writings is his analysis of how an offensive, especially when it has gone over to pursuit, can only go on so long — unless of course it can lead to complete victory — and that it is important not to overextend such pursuit or it can lead to a reversal of momentum and perhaps a major reversal of strength overall between the two contending forces.[71]

In the armed struggle in the U.S. a particular application of the offense within the defense will be necessary to deal especially with air attacks and even possible nuclear attacks on the strongholds of the revolutionary army: the tactical approach of fighting at close quarters (or "intermingled") with the enemy forces, at least in certain circumstances. Here we can also learn from our enemy — in particular the tactic, advocated by McNamara and some others, of quick thrusts into Eastern Europe with the start of war with the Soviet bloc, to "neutralize" at least some of battlefield nuclear war-fighting of the Warsaw Pact, as analyzed in the *Revolutionary Worker.*[72] At the same time we should even more learn from the policies developed by the leaders of our class, such as Mao's 1964 discussion of how to deal with the threat of atomic attacks on Chinese cities:

> We shall run away when they drop the atom bombs. When they enter the city, we shall also enter the city and the enemy

[71] There is also an analogy here to momentum — "runs" — in basketball: to the need to "consolidate" and maintain the advantage when the momentum of the "run" begins to be lost. When a team is on a run things go its way for awhile, but inevitably, by the laws of motion, it proves impossible to keep things up on that level; and if that team tries to keep the "run" on that level then it begins making mistakes — turnovers, etc. — and giving the advantage, or at least the opportunity to seize the advantage, back to the other side. We can learn from basketball as well as other aspects of life. I'm certainly not the one who'll be opposed to using basketball to learn! — and since the other side insists on continually using the military and war as a frame of reference for sports, for reactionary purposes, why shouldn't we draw lessons from sports to serve revolutionary struggles and aims? And the principles involved in this basketball example relate by analogy to the interpenetration of offense and defense in war.

[72] "Nuclear War Fighting With a Certified Dove," *RW*, No. 244, p. 10.

> will not dare to use the atom bomb. We shall engage in street fighting. At any rate, we shall fight them.[73]

There is in certain respects and up to a point an analogy between the forces of proletarian revolution, in particular where the armed struggle takes the form of insurrection followed by civil war, and what Mao says about the fascist states at the time around World War 2 — how important the offensive is to them, that they must remain on the offensive or be ruined and defeated.[74] But, as I said, this is in certain respects and up to a point; where this analogy breaks down is that it would be fundamentally wrong and harmful — and flying in the face of historical experience — to argue that revolutionary armed forces cannot fight from the strategic defensive and accumulate through fighting the basis to go over, sooner or later, to the strategic offensive and win ultimate victory. Whether a revolutionary war should (or must, to have a chance of success) begin from the strategic defensive or with a concerted offensive, as in the kind of insurrectionary armed struggle discussed up to this point, depends on the concrete conditions and differs with different countries (and in general terms with the two basic types of countries: imperialist states and oppressed nations, with insurrection followed by civil war the general model in the first type and protracted revolutionary war, beginning in the countryside and with the strategic defensive, generally the model in the second type). It is counterrevolutionary war that cannot be fought on a protracted basis on the strategic defensive (at least not by counterrevolutionary forces involved in war against revolutionary armed forces); and more generally all imperialists and reactionaries (and not just fascist states) have great difficulty sustaining a war where they cannot succeed in simply overpowering their enemy and where they have difficulty confronting him in fixed battle lines (this remains so despite the efforts of

[73] Mao, "Talk on Putting Military Affairs Work Into Full Effect and Cultivating Successors to the Revolution (June 16, 1964)," *Miscellany*, Part II, p. 356.

[74] See, for example, Mao, "The Turning Point in World War II," *MSW*, Vol. 3, p. 107.

the imperialists and reactionaries to employ more mobile forms of warfare).

But to return to the point of analogy with what Mao says about the fascist states around World War 2: these fascist states were, in fact, the "have not" imperialists, forced to seek a bigger sphere of influence and a bigger share in worldwide plunder and exploitation, especially in the colonies. They not only had the necessity, in the actual circumstances in which they found themselves, to seek a major redivision of the world to their advantage (as did the "have" imperialists of the time) but they had to adopt dramatic tactics of offense in the attempt to deliver crippling blows to their rivals before the strategically superior reserves of the latter could be brought into play. In a different way — and with profoundly different and opposite goals and overall means — the revolutionary proletariat, where its necessary strategic approach is to begin with armed insurrection, must also strike dramatic blows quickly. It must shatter the existing status quo and balance of forces, thus bringing into play its vast, powerful reserves — among the masses of the oppressed — and bringing over to its side important parts of the previous reserves and forces of the enemy, among his own troops as well as middle forces in society who tend to "go with the flow" (and more to the point, with the power — with who is on top or at least has the momentum).

But here, again, the analogy ends, because, after a certain phase, even if the insurrection is victorious, it will come to the point where consolidation of what has been won will be necessary (once more the relevance of the analysis by Clausewitz on pursuit coming to its limitations in any given situation). It is quite possible then that the newly established revolutionary regime will have to go over to the strategic defensive for a period in the civil war that follows.[75]

[75] In this light I have to modify my "correction" in *Conquer the World* to a statement in *Mao Tsetung's Immortal Contributions* in the chapter on revolutionary warfare. In this "correction" I underestimated the degree to which the importance of the defensive at the beginning of a war may apply to even revolutionary war in imperialist countries. This can be seen if it is kept in mind that the insurrectionary phase, which must be

The Prospects of Actually Winning

Yes, the other side *is* powerful — it does have a genuinely awesome arsenal of destruction — but it is also strategically vulnerable (Vietnam certainly showed that imperialism is not invincible!) and it is facing the unbelievably difficult prospect of world war (strategically even more difficult for it than for the international proletariat and revolutionary people worldwide). The present world situation, including the ever more intense "face-off" of the rival imperialist blocs, contains many elements favorable for the revolutionary proletariat and the masses of the oppressed in the world. Wars are never decided by weapons alone, and in the case of revolutionary war versus counterrevolutionary war this is all the more the case — or there never could or would have been a successful revolution![76]

The horror produced by the prospect of a war between the rival imperialist blocs — involving almost certainly the massive destruction of major nuclear exchanges — can itself be an impetus toward revolutionary struggle against the imperialists, and must be developed as such by the revolutionary communists. The horror produced by such a war, if it actually does break out — if it is not prevented by revolution — would be truly monstrous and devastating; but this does not change the overall

---

characterized by the offensive, is in a sense a prelude to civil war — a decisive stage and struggle in its own right, without whose success the revolutionary civil war cannot follow, but nevertheless a prelude to the civil war that will inevitably follow a successful insurrection and initial seizure of power. (Compare *Conquer the World*, pp. 31-34.)

[76] Even war waged by reactionary forces is never a "purely military" affair. For example, the victory of Caesar over Pompey in the civil war in ancient Rome was in large part due to political factors, including Caesar's use of political maneuvers and enticements to split and weaken the enemy army in combination with successful battlefield strategy and tactics. Or to take another example, the conquest of Mexico by Cortez involved not only the military aspect but also his tactics in pitting many of the peoples he conquered against each other, making use of rivalries and so on — which contrasts with the more crude tactics of Pizarro, conquerer of Peru, who was a more unembellished and "personally-interested" plunderer and who lost his head, literally, in a falling out with his fellow pillagers.

task at hand nor the truth that the overthrow and the elimination of all exploiting systems and relations is the only way to finally abolish such monstrosity. Nor certainly does it change the fact that they will be more vulnerable than ever before, that the whole global landscape — including of course the U.S. — will be suddenly, dramatically, and profoundly changed, one way or the other. Our basic orientation must remain that put forth by Mao in 1964:

> One must not become flustered in fighting with rifles, guns, or atom bombs. One will not become flustered if one is well prepared politically. . . . In general, we must be ready to fight, we must not become flustered when the fighting starts, we also must not be flustered in fighting the atom bomb. Do not be afraid. It is nothing but a big disorder throughout the world. It is nothing but people dying. Man eventually must die, he may die standing up or lying down. Those who do not die will go on with their work, if one-half meets with death, there is still another half. . . . Do not be afraid of imperialism. It will not do to be afraid, the more one is afraid, the less enthusiasm one will have. Being prepared and unafraid, one will have the enthusiasm.[77]

And I must say that after having gone deeply into and facing squarely this whole prospect of "nuclear winter" and the kind of devastation that I think you have to realize is on the agenda, if it's not prevented by revolution — after all that I still found it tremendously uplifting and inspiring to go back and read this statement by Mao which, despite the greatly increased destructiveness of nuclear weapons today as compared to 1964, embodies a fundamentally correct and vital, liberating orientation.

On the other hand, Mao also insisted that fighting on enthusiasm alone would lead to mistakes and specifically to being tricked by the enemy.[78] We must combine our revolutionary enthusiasm — our urgent desire for radical change and our deep

[77] Mao, "Cultivating Successors to the Revolution," *Miscellany*, Part II, p. 357.

[78] See Mao, "Problems of Strategy in China's Revolutionary War," *MSW*, Vol. 1, p. 188.

hatred and strategic contempt for imperialism and its crimes — with sober, serious, scientific, and consistent preparation for revolution. That means most of all political preparation now, but it also means specific preparation for revolutionary war — in the realm now of theory and strategic thinking and the urgent summing up of the practical experience in war of all different forces, but especially revolutionary forces, in the international arena. (One important form of this might be conducting interviews with and requesting letters from veterans who fought in the imperialist armed forces in Vietnam, or elsewhere, and people with experience in warfare *against* imperialism, from all over the world. This could be published and important lessons thus popularized.) It also means taking initiative and making innovations to develop practical steps which are not themselves military but involve people in mass forms that lay a basis for military organization in the future, when the armed struggle does come on the agenda. (Note that Sun Tzu, the expert on warfare in ancient China, stresses the importance of drill — even without arms — at the beginning of military training. His works exerted significant influence on Mao, among others, and are for good reason studied and applied by diverse forces to this day.)[79]

In short, without making rash mistakes and being tricked or provoked by the enemy on the basis of our own enthusiasm or impatience, we must prepare now to be able, as soon as conditions ripen and a political jolt or tremor in society opens a wide and deep enough crack, to channel the eruption of the formerly suppressed revolutionary energy of oppressed masses and launch and wage a revolutionary armed struggle. And when we do so it must be with the real perspective of going all out to win!

[79] See Sun Tzu, *The Art Of War*, translated with an introduction by Samuel B. Griffith (London: Oxford University Press, 1980).

QUESTIONS ESPECIALLY CONCERNING THE CARRYING OUT OF THE PARTY'S CENTRAL TASK TODAY

More on the Question of Lagging the Objective Conditions

There is a fundamental aspect of truth — and great importance — to our insistence (beginning especially in the 1979-80 period) that we are seriously lagging the objective situation and the needs of the revolutionary movement — as opposed to the notion (and the accusation frequently hurled at us by opportunists) that we are "too far out in front of things."[80] The fact is that the development of the crisis of the imperialist system, and in particular the moves toward war of the imperialists (on both sides), are far outstripping the revolutionary movement, and the communist vanguard forces are seriously lagging in relation to this, not only in the U.S. but internationally. Especially when viewed in connection with the urgent question of preventing world war through revolution, this is a very serious problem to be attacked.

On the other hand, it is important to divide the objective conditions faced by the communist vanguard into two interrelated but separate aspects: the development of the crisis and developments in the enemy camp generally (most especially the accelerating moves toward war) and on the other hand the mood of the masses and their level of political understanding and activity at any given time. The first aspect is the most important and in an overall sense the one that determines the mood and political consciousness and struggle of the masses. But this must not be taken mechanically — and here it is important to

[80] See, for example, Avakian, *Coming From Behind to Make Revolution and Crucial Questions in Coming From Behind.*

stress again what was emphasized in the last Central Committee Report of our party: "periods of preparation in one country are periods of revolution in another." Such revolutions are also a part, indeed a very significant and influential part, of the objective situation and greatly affect the sentiments of the masses in all parts of the world and their level of political consciousness and struggle. All in all, in this aspect of the mood, political consciousness, and activity of the masses (and speaking specifically of the U.S.), the question of lagging the objective conditions is more complicated and contradictory.

In 1979-80 when we began really stressing this question of lagging there were new and inspiring revolutionary upsurges in several countries — including Nicaragua and Iran, where unfortunately revolutionary mass struggles have not led to the establishment of revolutionary regimes but have seen power usurped by new reactionary elements (in "revolutionary" disguise) dependent on imperialism and serving its interests. There was also at that time more of a mood of ferment and rebellion in the U.S. itself. In the last few years — despite recent and even more inspiring examples of revolutionary struggle in other countries (in particular in Peru) — the overall effect of the international situation and of conditions in the U.S. has temporarily produced a suffocating political atmosphere in the U.S. This has tended to suppress protest and rebellion or channel discontent into well-trod and "safe" paths of reformism (even though there have been important instances and outbreaks of protest and rebellion in the U.S., such as the Miami rebellions and the increasingly militant protests against war preparations). But most fundamentally, this situation, including the contradictory moods and sentiments among the masses, involving both outrage and despair in the face of increasingly desperate circumstances and seemingly overwhelming powers bent on destruction — this is precisely a *lull before the storm*, a lull full of tension signaling explosion in the future, perhaps the very near future.

The last Central Committee Report of our party speaks to this question — the different aspects of the objective situation and their interrelation.[81] It is necessary to return to and focus on this, so that precisely with the urgent task of racing to catch up to the situation of crisis and especially the growing threat of world war, our political work to "come from behind" can take more fully into account and deal with the contradictory moods and trends among the masses and their underlying basis. The point is not to tail the backward or be immobilized ourselves by the present political passivity still characteristic of the majority of the masses, but to bring forward the advanced and train them as revolutionary leaders and exert a revolutionary influence as broadly among the masses as possible now, preparing to win to the revolutionary position and revolutionary struggle many, many times that number as things approach and then reach an exploding point, in one way or another. In order to correctly handle this, it is crucial to keep in mind both aspects of the objective conditions and changes within them, and at the same time to continue to strategically base our work on the understanding that the leading and determining aspect is the development of the overall world situation (including crisis and war preparations and also revolutionary struggles) which, despite its intimidating and demoralizing effects on many, will nevertheless force growing numbers of people into motion and with sudden leaps and dramatic turns will jolt millions suddenly into political life and struggle.

Revolutionary Intellectuals, the Advanced Minority, and a Revolutionary Mass Movement

The advanced, politically conscious forces — including the revolutionary intellectuals who are generally the first to take up revolutionary theory and begin developing a revolutionary line, as well as the advanced among the masses who rally to it and take it up as their own — are always a small minority in society,

[81] See *Accumulating Revolutionary Forces for the Coming Showdown.*

especially in "normal" (nonrevolutionary) times. (And I think this basically applies to socialist society as well.) This is nothing to get upset or disoriented about — even now, with the urgent tasks at hand and monumental stakes involved. The point is that the passive posture of large numbers of the masses can and will change dramatically and virtually overnight with the approach and especially the eruption of a revolutionary crisis, when "all of a sudden" millions can be rallied — though they do not "automatically" rally — to the proletarian revolutionary banner. Lenin did not shrink from describing this phenomenon as one where "millions come to the assistance of a few score of Party people" (a statement worth pondering).[82] This strengthens our understanding of why it is so crucial not to give vent to frustration — perhaps leading to adventurism — but to consistently carry out the work of political preparation to be in the strongest position for the time when millions of such "reserves" do "come to our assistance," perhaps very suddenly.

Linked closely to this point (though not completely identical with it) is the role of the theoretical work and breakthroughs (the rupturing of rusty revisionist and reformist shackles) our party and others have made in the last few years, which have been crucial in preparing the ground and making the political terrain more favorable for the development of a revolutionary movement of masses (a point also stressed in our party's last Central Committee Report). Here there is an analogy with what Mao summed up about the Russian Revolution:

> Ideologically, politically, and organizationally the Bolshevik-Menshevik split prepared the way for the victory of the October Revolution. And without the Bolsheviks' struggle against the Mensheviks and the revisionism of the Second International, the October Revolution could never have triumphed.[83]

[82] Lenin, "Third All-Russia Congress of Soviets of Workers', Soldiers' and Peasants' Deputies (January 10-18, 1918)," *LCW*, Vol. 26, p. 459.

[83] Mao Tsetung, *A Critique of Soviet Economics*, translated by Moss Roberts (New York and London: Monthly Review Press, 1977), p. 36.

The present period is a kind of pivot in the process of building on those theoretical breakthroughs. This is in line with the emphasis in the party's last Central Committee Report on making the line of our party (and this applies now to the *Declaration of the Revolutionary Internationalist Movement* as well!) more accessible to the masses, of entering more boldly and broadly into different arenas of mass struggle and political ferment, armed with, applying, and popularizing this line.

Within all this there is a particular and crucial role for the advanced from among the basic masses themselves, as "links" or "levers" to spread this line and unleash the politically conscious activism of many others among the basic masses. This is important now and its importance will be magnified many times over as things develop — and especially when they do reach the point of a revolutionary crisis. This is not a refutation of the principle that Lenin stressed in *What Is To Be Done?* that what is needed is professional revolutionaries, regardless of whether they come from among the intellectuals or the workers; but it is a recognition of the different roles that different people can and must play in the revolutionary movement — whether as professional revolutionaries (i.e., full-time party workers) or basic party members. And more fundamentally it is a recognition of the distinction between revolutionary intellectuals, or even an advanced minority composed of revolutionary intellectuals and basic masses, on the one hand, and a revolutionary movement of the masses on the other. It is a recognition of the particular, and in important aspects pivotal, role the advanced from among the basic masses can play, especially as the objective conditions develop and ripen, in making the transition — or leap — from the one to the other: from an advanced force, with the party at the core, involving a small minority while influencing broader numbers, to a vanguard actually winning and leading millions in class struggle going over to its highest form, the armed struggle for political power.

Further on the Importance of Party-Building

That the importance of building the party in all aspects — including bringing into the party many fresh forces from among the basic masses — is also magnified many times over by the urgent tasks facing us (by "what time it is" on the historical agenda and the stakes involved) should not be surprising. There is not only the general principle that there must be a vanguard party to lead a revolution — particularly a proletarian revolution — in every sphere; but more specifically, if there is to be any chance to influence and divert masses hurled into motion by the dramatic sharpening of the objective world situation, to influence and divert them to a proletarian revolutionary position, then the party's roots and its influence must grow and deepen many, many times over in the period just ahead.

This is possible, but it cannot happen without advanced people joining up (why not — if confused and ignorant people among the masses are joining the imperialist army out of desperation, why can't the enlightened, politically advanced join the party of the proletariat?) and carrying out systematic party work according to a single strategy and plan and an overall division of labor facilitating the most effective revolutionary activity. Taking part in the political life of the party and the ideological struggle within it; being trained as a conscious revolutionary on the one hand while at the same time contributing to both spreading the political influence and building the organized strength of the party among oppressed proletarians and other oppressed masses; and contributing to further developing and enriching that line: to what degree new, vital forces, especially among the basic masses, step forward to do this could be crucial in enabling revolutionary roots to be too strong to be blown away or torn up in the storms ahead — even if the party structure *is* temporarily disrupted or shattered (a vital point discussed earlier in relation to ordinary people rising to the occasion in extraordinary times). This could be crucial too in making it possible for massive revolutionary forces to spring up when the conditions ripen.

Imperialism and the Seal of Parasitism

Lenin, in *Imperialism, The Highest Stage of Capitalism*, refers to the "extraordinary growth of a class, or rather, of a stratum of rentiers, i.e., people who live by 'clipping coupons,' who take no part in any enterprise whatever, whose profession is idleness," and he sums up that "the export of capital, one of the most essential economic bases of imperialism, still more completely isolates the rentiers from production and *sets the seal of parasitism on the whole country that lives by exploiting the labor of several overseas countries and colonies.*"[84] At that time Lenin cited England as the paramount example of such parasitism (and it certainly has not gotten less parasitic since then!). But today it is the U.S. that provides the most outstanding example of parasitic world exploiter and pillager.

It is not only the case that broad strata within the U.S. (of the petty bourgeoisie and of the working class as well) have for several decades (since the last world war) received significant droppings from the spoils of international robbery, but it is also a fact that the soldiers in the U.S. armed forces are after all the soldiers of empire, many of them directly stationed in other countries and particularly in the colonies (or neocolonies) playing the role of an occupying army, able and encouraged to act like thugs and lord it over the people (even now it is rare to find a "my true story as a U.S. soldier in Vietnam" novel that does not refer to the Vietnamese, all Vietnamese, as "gooks" and other similar terms of endearment and respect). And more generally, there is a broad (if often vague) awareness among the people in the U.S. — even reaching down to the lower strata to some degree — of not only "living better" than just about everyone else in the world (a

[84] Lenin, *Imperialism, The Highest Stage of Capitalism*, *LCW*, Vol. 22, p. 277, emphasis added.

fact constantly drummed into people through the media, etc.) but also living *at the expense* of large numbers of people in the world (a fact less frequently and systematically discussed in the popular media, though at times and especially of late there seems to be more of this — to more explicitly remind people "what you have to defend").

Further, all this strongly influences even how people respond to the increased hardship being experienced by many (for example the "Buy American" and other jingoistic responses to unemployment which no small number of people gravitate toward). The widespread malaise among the middle classes (and sections of better-off workers) is also an expression of the disorientation and demoralization of strata whose lives and lifestyles have been shaped by a significant involvement with the "seal of parasitism" that is "set upon the whole country." While the undermining of traditional morality definitely has its positive aspects, this whole phenomenon, including the depth of corruption and demoralization (demoralization in a double sense, meaning not just discouragement or despair but the loss of a sense of a coherent morality) among broad strata, also poses a significant problem for the revolutionary movement in the U.S. in that it can provide fertile soil for reactionary mass mobilization — and actual fighting forces — in the service of imperialism and against revolution.

On the other hand, all this stresses the importance of basing the revolutionary movement on and building the party's most solid foundation among those oppressed proletarians with the least stake in the present order, those who are objectively, and who feel themselves, victims of this system and can readily identify with others who are oppressed — even more — throughout the world. It is not that such proletarians in the U.S. have literally and absolutely no part or no share in the parasitism and the spoils of imperialism (it would be very difficult to find any such people in the U.S.!) but that this is more than outweighed by the exploitation and oppression they suffer, their hatred for life under this system, and their desire not to see "America number one again" but to see a different kind of world without everything that America stands for. These are people who gravitate toward and when given the chance will eagerly take up the position of *welcoming* the defeats and setbacks suffered by U.S. imperialism and of utilizing them to build a revolutionary struggle as part of the world revolutionary struggle of the international proletariat.

The experience of the '60s in the U.S. in the context of the international struggle against imperialism (in particular U.S. imperialism), with forces from among the basic proletariat and other oppressed masses rising up — in particular Black people but other oppressed nationalities and other social movements as well — holds many valuable lessons. Even though this was not a situation where a proletarian vanguard was at the head and a proletarian line and outlook in the lead, this experience shows the potential for revolutionary struggle in the U.S. in the period ahead, including the potential for influencing even the more privileged strata — on the basis of a revolutionary section of the proletariat, with our party as its vanguard, stepping forcefully onto the political stage. It is a truly remarkable thing, given the depth and breadth of parasitism in the U.S., that in the '60s so many turned so strongly against "their own" imperialism and a significant number even supported (what was then) a revolutionary force in defeating U.S. imperialism in Vietnam. A truly wonderful thing!

Even though the '80s are and will be more complex and more difficult — and harder times, especially given such parasitism, can lead to a more narrow and backward reaction among some strata (as noted) — still the strategic possibilities for influencing, for winning (at least to "friendly neutrality") broad numbers of people, including among the more privileged workers and middle-class strata, will be greater in the period ahead than in the '60s. But, besides the development of the objective situation, this depends on the work of the party and the stand and actions of the basic proletarians, especially the advanced among them, not only when the situation reaches the point of acute crisis deeply convulsing all of society but from here toward that point.

Again on the United Front Strategy and the Crucial Element of Proletarian Leadership

It is a general principle and is especially true in politically quiescent (dead) times that within the proletariat itself the advanced need a politicized atmosphere — air to breathe — in order to sustain revolutionary activity. They need to be involved with and influencing many different social movements of different strata (this too is addressed in some depth in the party's last Central Committee Report).

At any given time the involvement of such advanced proletarians — especially as such, as a social force of class-conscious proletarians — in these various social movements, their uniting with people from other strata but also their "injecting" proletarian politics and the proletarian outlook into such movements will not only give them more air to breathe but will exert a powerful influence on these movements and more broadly in society. It will push forward the whole process of developing the strategic approach of a united front under proletarian leadership, including by bringing more forces among the proletariat itself into motion, into political life and action. And as a crucial part of this it will give impetus to and provide more fertile soil for building and strengthening the party and its roots among the oppressed proletarians. The growing involvement and influence of a force of class-conscious proletarians within the major social movements is a kind of a key link that we have to take hold of to accelerate the development of the whole process of building the revolutionary movement and wielding the strategic weapon of the united front under proletarian leadership.[85]

All this is an expression of the fact that, although the class struggle is the essence of politics (in class-divided society) and

[85] In less developed form, and along with some primitive understanding and even certain erroneous tendencies, this basic point was spoken to way back in *Red Papers 2* of the Revolutionary Union — 15 years ago — and it not only remains true in its essential thrust but is also of heightened importance now.

the proletariat must be the leading, driving force in the revolutionary struggle against imperialism and all exploiting systems and relations, the strategy for proletarian revolution is not "class against class" but the united front under proletarian leadership. As Lenin hammered home in *What Is To Be Done?* (and elsewhere), the proletariat cannot develop its class consciousness,

> unless the workers learn to observe from concrete, and above all from topical (current), political facts and events, *every* other social class and *all* the manifestations of the intellectual, ethical and political life of these classes; unless they learn to apply in practice the materialist analysis and the materialist estimate of *all* aspects of the life and activity of *all* classes, strata and groups of the population.[86]

And, it can be added, consistent with Lenin's thrust here and his overall approach: unless the class-conscious proletariat learns to unite and struggle with other strata among the people and win and lead them in the revolutionary struggle. This, in turn, is a reflection of the fact that the goal of the class-conscious proletariat must not be revenge against the existing ruling class and the "right" to install itself as a new exploiting class but the establishment of the dictatorship of the proletariat as a transition to the abolition of the social basis for the division of society into classes and the transformation of society and the people to achieve classless communist society.

The United Front *on the Basis of* an Advanced Position Taken and Pole Established by the Party

Mao makes clear that in the Chinese Revolution at various stages (including in the stage of united front against Japan), without the armed forces commanded by the Communist Party

[86] Lenin, *What Is To Be Done?* (Peking: Foreign Languages Press, 1975), p. 86.

and the liberated base areas, it would not have been possible for the party to enter into and build the united front without losing its independence and initiative and giving up the prospect of leading such a united front.[87] There is, I believe, an analogy here to the present situation faced by our party in the U.S. (Note, especially for those in the political police of the enemy who snap to attention every time they see any reference, in whatever context and with whatever meaning, to armed struggle: I am saying there is an *analogy* here, with *political implications*, not a direct application of what Mao says to the military sphere in the U.S. at this time.) The analogy I'm making is this: it is precisely and only by establishing a clear-cut revolutionary stand and revolutionary pole in U.S. society and consistently working to rally the advanced, especially among the proletariat, to this pole, that it will be possible to apply the united front strategy correctly. It is only thus that other strata and forces with which it is correct and strategically necessary to seek unity will feel inclined and/or compelled to enter into a united front with us; and only thus that the strategic interests of the proletariat will be upheld and the prospect of proletarian leadership of the united front, infusing it with a clear-cut revolutionary thrust and content, will be maintained.[88] On this basis, and with this as a firm orientation, the question must be addressed of what it means in concrete political terms for the class-conscious proletariat to give leadership to the united front. First, it must be stressed that such leadership is concentrated through the role of the party and is impossible without that vanguard role. With that in mind, besides what is said in the *New Programme* of our party on this

[87] See, for example, Mao, "Problems of War and Strategy," *MSW*, Vol. 2, pp. 222, 225-26, and "On Tactics Against Japanese Imperialism," *MSW*, Vol. 1, pp. 166-67.

[88] This is another aspect of the point addressed in the party's Central Committee Report, on the need to "maintain a constant tension between the vanguard's fundamental need to be 'way out on a limb,' engaging the enemy in battle (as defined by our central task, which means political battle for us now) and, secondarily, the need to have that 'string tied to our backs,' building united fronts, never being completely cut off from the broad masses" (*Accumulating Revolutionary Forces for the Coming Showdown*, p. 6).

question,[89] the following statement by Mao has important application, especially in a period such as this where we are giving increased emphasis to entering into significant arenas of mass protest and rebellion and striving to influence them:

> How does the proletariat give political leadership through its party to all the revolutionary classes in the country? First, by putting forward basic political slogans that accord with the course of historical development and by putting forward slogans of action for each stage of development and each major turn of events in order to translate these political slogans into reality.[90]

Don't Overdo It, But Pay Correct Attention

In "Pay Attention to the Day to Day Needs of the Masses — But Don't Overdo It!" I argued strongly (and correctly) against a longstanding article of faith within the international communist movement (to call it religious conviction would hardly be an exaggeration) that the starting point and pivot of communist activity (at the time of the founding of our party, in falling into this error ourselves, we referred to it as the "center of gravity") must be involvement in the concerns and struggles of the masses around their day to day conditions and needs. I specifically refuted the frequent attempts to misuse Mao's insistence that, in the course of waging revolutionary war in China, the Communist Party and the government in the base areas must pay close attention to the day to day needs of the masses and help them solve their pressing economic problems. I pointed out that Mao first made clear that waging the revolutionary war was central and then, on that basis, urged attention to these day to day problems of the masses, and that it is an inversion (and perver-

[89] See *New Programme and New Constitution of the Revolutionary Communist Party, USA* (Chicago: RCP Publications, 1981), pp. 22-40, especially pp. 39-40.

[90] Mao, "The Tasks of the Chinese Communist Party in the Period of Resistance to Japan," *MSW*, Vol. 1, p. 274.

sion) of Mao's whole line to use his statements on this to justify a position that says first, before and as the basis for any other, higher form of political work or struggle, we must pay attention to the day to day needs of the masses. With regard to the situation and work of our party, I argued that the analogy is to the carrying out of our central task: "'Create Public Opinion . . . Seize Power' with agitation and propaganda central now and exposure as the key link." For us, that is what's central and ". . . in *that* context, and grasping *that* as the overall and essential thing that we are doing, then we have to pay attention to, or be conscious of, the problems and everyday needs of the masses. I mean that in the sense that we have to take them into account in carrying out our work."[91] It is for these reasons that this particular article (chapter in the pamphlet) was entitled "Pay Attention to the Day to Day Needs of the Masses — But Don't Overdo It!"

At this time, having established the correct orientation on this question, as expressed in that article (chapter), it is important to stress again that we must after all pay attention, correctly, to the day to day conditions and needs of the masses, especially the masses of oppressed proletarians. This is a point that is discussed in the party's last Central Committee Report, specifically in terms of exposure: "Speaking of the paper, it is important (and not at all economist) to include in our press exposures that powerfully lay bare the conditions and life experiences of proletarians in the U.S."[92] And the *Declaration of the Revolutionary Internationalist Movement*, while polemicizing against economism and exposing its main features, also correctly argues:

> It is not possible to build the revolutionary movement and lead it to victory without paying attention to the battles

[91] Bob Avakian, *If There Is to Be Revolution, There Must Be a Revolutionary Party* (Chicago: RCP Publications, 1982), p. 49; see also Mao, "Be Concerned with the Well-Being of the Masses, Pay Attention to Methods of Work," *MSW*, Vol. 1, pp. 147-52.

[92] *Accumulating Revolutionary Forces for the Coming Showdown*, p. 11.

> for daily existence of the working class and masses of other strata. While the party must not direct its own or the masses' attention mainly to such struggle nor foster the dissipation of its own and the masses' forces and energies on them, neither can the party fail to do work in relation to them. Leading economic struggles is not the same thing as economism. The proletarian party should take these struggles, especially those with the potential to go beyond conventional bounds, seriously into account. This means conducting work in relation to these struggles in such a way as to facilitate the moving of the masses to revolutionary positions, especially as the conditions for revolution ripen.[93]

It *is* true that without such an approach it will not be possible to build the revolutionary movement and lead it to victory, and it is also true that the more things sharpen up and especially as broader masses are suddenly jolted into resistance and political activity, work in relation to economic struggles (as outlined in the above statement from the *Declaration of the Revolutionary Internationalist Movement*) will assume more, not less, importance for building the revolutionary movement — *provided* it is actually done on such a correct basis, as a secondary if important part of the overall political work to build the revolutionary movement and prepare for the armed insurrection. In this sense, we can say, as a companion to the title of that chapter: Don't Overdo It, But Pay Correct Attention.

Their Ideological Offensive and Our Counteroffensive

Especially after being in France for awhile — where to a large and sickening extent politics is still presented, especially by the "Left," in terms of democracy versus fascism — I came to the point of concluding that an important first step politically would

[93] *Declaration of the Revolutionary Internationalist Movement*, p. 42.

be to abolish these two words.[94] But having kept up with the scene in the U.S. and observing the political and ideological atmosphere being created there of late, I am leaning toward the conclusion that it would be wrong to bury the word "fascist" at least. I say this despite the fact that my revulsion at the use of this term by much of the "Left" is certainly well-founded, and despite the crude flinging about of this term historically (and down to today) and the often grotesque errors and political deviations that have generally been associated with this. Still, even being "removed" from the scene in the U.S., it is impossible to observe that scene without being struck by the very real elements of fascism that are being built up in the political and ideological superstructure in particular.

This is particularly striking in the ideological, and more specifically, the cultural sphere. The cult of the body (the revolutionary proletariat certainly needs to stress being in condition for general health reasons and more specifically for the arduous revolutionary struggle ahead, but just as certainly not with the core of love for Self and for The Nation as a race of Supermen – and Superwomen, even if they still have to remain the subordinates of the Supermen) that screams out in this "let's get physical" craze; the cult of the military; the many-sided attack – including literal physical and sexual assault as well as the incessant preaching of wifely and motherly duty – to force women, even women with "responsibility outside the home," more firmly into a subordinate, debased, and brutalized position; the cult of the nation, including the revival of the U.S. as god's chosen nation (or at least as enjoying "favored nation status" with him); the promotion, from the highest levels of government, of the "Moral Majority" and generally of obscurantist-jingoistic mythology and ritual; and along with all this the drumbeat of the will to triumph: these are some of the major aspects of what I would

[94] Though I didn't put it in exactly these terms, this was very much on my mind in writing "And What Should We Call the *Third* Time? or Still Fighting the Battles of the 19th Century at the Approach of the 21st," as part of *More Reflections and Sketches*, *RW*, 206 (May 20, 1983), p. 3.

have to call a genuinely fascist element within the ideological offensive of the U.S. imperialists in this period.

This is precisely not some "classless" or "systemless" phenomenon that can be attributed merely to the fact that evil people are in positions of power (though that is certainly true, it is also certainly *not* an *exception* to the rule). Rather it is an expression of the necessity that the U.S. imperialist ruling class as a whole faces, a necessity in the ideological realm — reflecting and addressing their necessity in the practical-material world — a necessity especially to fan the fires of blind jingoism, to dazzle people with individual and collective (national) narcissism and prepare them for the orgy of death and destruction that is the epitome of the program for "USA-No. 1," and at the same time to overwhelm and intimidate those who aren't swept up in this, who won't go along or who actually resist. It is not necessarily the case that the U.S. imperialists will have to implement an actual fascist form of their bourgeois dictatorship, that is, a dictatorship openly based on systematic terror within the U.S. itself. But in any case things in the U.S. will get much more repressive, in terms of the atmosphere created as well as the brute force employed by the apparatus of the state (police, army, courts, etc.), and the fascist elements within their ideological offensive that I have pointed to will be an important part of all that.

In this light it is very instructive to look at the main points raised in a well thought out response to "American Patriotism — A Challenge." In that article I challenged "anyone to give an explanation of why they are patriotic Americans or why patriotism for the USA is a good thing, which cannot be shown to come down to a statement of why they want to perpetuate a situation where they have a position of privilege — relatively greater or lesser, but privilege all the same — at the expense of, and at the cost of tremendous suffering on the part of, the great majority of people in the world."[95]

The author of this response centers his arguments around

[95] See "Provocations," *RW*, No. 228, p. 4.

the idea that as a result of Vietnam and Watergate "Americans have nothing left to believe in. America has by and large become an alienated, morally bankrupt nation that can believe in little but video games, sex, and a frail sense of machismo." His conclusion is not that this shows the urgent need for a revolution that is directed against everything America has more clearly been revealed to stand for, but that "above all, Americans need something to believe in, something for which they will be willing to sacrifice. This is a function that can be fulfilled by patriotism."

It certainly can! — and here lies the essence of the problem. The writer does not realize it, but his position plays directly into the hands of the U.S. imperialists and their drive to unite the American Nation around something very specific to believe in: the need to create the conditions where America will reign unchallenged in the world (or what's left of it) — which means nothing less than world war and everything that involves. Like many who today are seeking (and others who have previously sought) to solve the ills and cure the evils of America on a liberal-democratic basis, without a radical transformation of the whole society and its values, this writer raises the notion that the U.S. has failed to live up to the ideals upon which it is based. This is an argument I addressed in the article "*Declaration of Independence*, Equal Opportunity, and Bourgeois Right,"[96] where I pointed out that the U.S. has in fact lived up to the principles and ideals on which it was founded — insofar as that is actually possible — and the inevitable result involves the very things that this writer and many other like-minded people abhor. But this response concludes by arguing:

> If only we can learn to live according to these ideals, we can once again be proud of America, not because of its fabulous wealth and military prowess, but because of its moral superiority. This is a patriotism that will do no one any harm. Rather, it will serve to once again provide inspiration

[96] See "*Declaration of Independence*, Equal Opportunity, and Bourgeois Right," *RW*, No. 230 (November 11, 1983), p. 3.

> for the millions who continue to fight for justice throughout the world.

However well-meaning this might be, the fact is that there is no basis whatsoever for America to have "moral superiority" in the world (and the use of the word "superiority" here is a sign that something is wrong even if the intentions are good). America's "fabulous wealth and military prowess" are a product and integral part of American imperialist plunder worldwide and are founded in exploitation and misery historically and internationally: it is this which America embodies and symbolizes for "the millions who continue to fight for justice throughout the world." And those millions, far from drawing inspiration from America and its ideals, face America as a major obstacle and ruthless enemy. Was it somehow accidental that the Vietnamese people had to wage revolutionary war against the U.S. and its allies for three decades to finally drive them out, or that oppressed peoples throughout the world face the same task today?[97] In sharp opposition to what the writer argues, patriotism for America, of any kind — even the most "idealistic," harkening back to the principles of the *Declaration of Independence* and so on — will do a great deal of harm to the vast majority of people in the world and indeed to humanity as a whole, especially given what is now coming on the world agenda. The USA is an oppressor country — in fact right now it is "Number One" among oppressor countries in the world and is trying to "keep it that way," with everything that means. Patriotism for America is patriotism for *that* — and can be nothing else.

The writer does recognize, after all, that there is a basic inconsistency in his arguments. He acknowledges, "Of course, in what you call 'the spirit of internationalism,' you may argue in

[97] As for Ho Chi Minh's use of a passage from the *Declaration of Independence* in declaring Vietnam's independence from France at the end of World War 2 — a fact this writer cites — that is, unfortunately, an example of weaknesses and limitations in the Vietnamese Revolution and its leadership, *not* an indication of the value of the *Declaration of Independence* for revolutionary struggle in today's world.

response that Americans should feel concern not only for Americans, but for all people of the world. In this way, one can claim that patriotism will have the bad effect of making Americans feel compassion only for their fellow citizens. This is a valid argument, but it is a bit unrealistic." Why? Because, he says, "It is difficult to feel compassion for those we cannot understand and who are in addition hostile towards us."

Here the writer falls into a series of contradictory notions and feelings, which combine some sense that people have reason to hate America for what it has done in the world with at best an incredibly naive clinging to long-since exposed myths, like the idea that "good, honest, compassionate young Americans join organizations such as the Peace Corps in an honest attempt to help the world's poor, only to often be regarded as nasty American imperialists. . . ." Now, I would not deny that, especially at first (in the early '60s), many people did join the Peace Corps with such motivation, but has this writer really never heard of the many returned Peace Corps volunteers who learned what their real role was to be and who exposed the Peace Corps as in fact an arm of "nasty American imperialists" and their exploitation and oppression throughout the Third World?

At bottom this writer senses that something is fundamentally wrong with America but, still believing in its ideals, and its mythology, he seeks to cure the sickness with a watered-down version of the same "medicine" that the U.S. imperialists and their unleashed social base are trumpeting, from the White House to the Moral Majority, from Walter Mondale, Gary Hart, and Tip O'Neill to Jesse Jackson. If the fight is kept on this terrain the imperialists are bound to win, and they will turn to their service all attempts to center the fight there and wage it on the terms of who is the best patriot, what is real American patriotism.

What this writer fundamentally fails to grasp is not only the desirability of proletarian revolution — as part of the world revolutionary movement — to overthrow America (which is and can only be the same thing as U.S. imperialism), but also the fact that the deep signs of sickness that he cites and agonizes over are an indication of the ripening possibilities for a radical cure. This does mean the possibility of a radical right-wing "solution," it is true, but also of a revolution from the "left," or rather from the bottom: a revolution led by the proletariat to spring into the air and overturn all existing social conditions and relations and establish whole new ones and *their* corresponding values and ideals. Thus, when the writer argues that a resurgence of patriotism in the U.S. — of the kind he advocates — is "certainly better than the current situation in which people care for nothing but themselves" and in any case it is "about the best we can hope for at this moment," he is profoundly wrong.

All this emphasizes the importance of our waging a determined counteroffensive in the ideological sphere, straight up against their offensive, with what could be considered its guiding themes: "Being U.S. Imperialism Means Never Having To Say You're Sorry," and "Let's Get Back To Doing It Like We Used To Do — But More and With a Vengeance." Waging such an ideological counteroffensive means not only continuing and deepening exposure of their ideological offensive (as well as all-around exposure of the imperialist system and what it is bringing on the agenda now) but boldly raising the banner of proletarian revolution and stepping out right in their face, ideologically and politically. It means finding creative ways to expose their lackeys and "models" (and their revival of racist and sexist stereotypes) to sharp ridicule. It also means making clear, even proclaiming — aggressively but calmly, without hype or frenzy — that we have the line and program, the orientation and strategy, and the leadership to actually do what we are calling for when the opening is created.

I have discussed how right now is a difficult period in many ways, especially for the advanced, and in this light we should not only keep in mind but popularize what Mao emphasized during the Great Leap Forward in China, in the face of a torrent of opposition from bourgeois forces, including within the party: "If you want others to stand firm, you must first stand firm yourselves. If you want other people not to waver, you must not waver yourself."[98] Standing firm and boldly carrying out an ideological counteroffensive is a vital part of being able to unleash and rally many others who also hate all this but feel suffocated and intimidated.

Popularizing the Question of the Armed Struggle for Power

It is not time to raise the armed struggle for power as an immediate practical question in the U.S., but *it is* time to raise preparation for that struggle as an immediate, urgent, and imminently (as well as eminently) practical question. By this I mean not only the kind of political preparation spoken to repeatedly but also more specific political/organizational preparation more directly linked to developing a mass consciousness about the possibility and also the strategic orientation, means, and methods for carrying out this armed struggle when it does become an immediate practical question.

Besides the aspect of developing in this period mass forms that are not in themselves of a military character but could be transformed into such when the armed struggle is on the agenda (a point spoken to earlier), there is the need to popularize among the oppressed proletarians and other masses — and especially the advanced among them — the orientation of viewing and participating in everything, all major world events and struggles in society, in terms of how this will influence things toward and contribute to the armed insurrection (and civil war) when the opportunity does ripen. Raising and popularizing this now and in an ongoing way — even when and even though the form of struggle we must be focusing our efforts on now is political and not military struggle — is an indispensable part of overall preparation for the armed struggle: for the shift in emphasis to the "seize power" aspect of our central task.

[98] Mao Tsetung, "Speech at the Lushan Conference (July 23, 1959)," in Stuart Schram, ed., *Chairman Mao Talks to the People* (New York: Pantheon Books, 1974), p. 139.

More on "Desperate Risings of the Masses"

In *Charting the Uncharted Course* we noted that in defending the "taking to arms" of the revolutionary masses in the 1905 Revolution in Russia and looking forward to a future revolutionary uprising (which did occur in 1917 and was successful), Lenin called attention to the fact that "Marx was also able to appreciate that there are moments in history when a desperate struggle of the *masses* even in a hopeless cause *is essential* for the further schooling of these masses and their training for the *next* struggle." Applying the basic point to the situation in the U.S., *Charting* goes on to say:

> We may be confronted with the situation of trying to "turn a 1905 into a 1917." The '60s have played a kind of 1905-type role in this country though as we pointed out they never got fully to the scale of a dress rehearsal struggle for power. But perhaps something that starts off looking like it will not succeed, looking as though the necessary forces are not in the fray, will require us to support it, lead it, seek to broaden it into a successful attempt. . . . An insurrection is not a rebellion, or even many rebellions. But it is possible that under turbulent overall conditions, perhaps world war, that maybe the fifth rebellion could be the spark for an insurrectionary attempt.[99]

And we should add "or perhaps the imminent possibility of and dramatic moves toward world war or in this context a particular military action or 'adventure' of U.S. imperialism" as other possible scenarios of "turbulent overall conditions."

The emphasis that must be placed on the prevention of world war through revolution gives added significance to the points cited just above from *Charting*. It heightens the need for the vanguard to be "tense" to the possibility of turning rebellions

[99] *Charting the Uncharted Course*, p. 13; the quote by Lenin is also on p. 13 of *Charting* and is from Lenin, "Preface to Russian Translation of the Letters of Karl Marx to Dr. Kugelman," *Marx Engels Marxism* (Peking: Foreign Languages Press, 1978), p. 210.

and overall upheaval and turmoil in society into an actual attempt at armed insurrection with a perspective of giving this an organized and coordinated character and carrying it through to win — *before* world war is unleashed. But this can only have a chance of success — and in any case contribute to the advance of the revolutionary movement in the U.S. and worldwide — if we are talking about a real rising of *masses* — and not some outburst of frustrated revolutionary intellectuals or of a small force with no political connections with masses, especially with the advanced among the oppressed proletarians, which would have no prospect of becoming a real uprising of masses.

From another angle, this underscores that our work of preparation now (as discussed throughout this book) can play a vital part in creating the kind of political "tenseness" among the masses that would enable them to respond with a revolutionary uprising to some sudden and dramatic turn in world events and in the functioning of U.S. society itself. Of course it is impossible to precisely predict or preplan all this in detail, and it is quite possible, as we have stressed in *Charting*, that it is a spontaneous uprising of masses that "sounds the call" for the overall revolutionary insurrection — sounds it at least for those with ears to hear. (In this regard it is important to recall not only what is cited above from *Charting* but also the remarks by Engels quoted by Stalin [and cited in footnote 61] that an uprising, "even if begun in a brainless way," may be transformable into a successful revolutionary armed struggle.)

This is a further illustration — and highlighting — of the fact that the party's central task, create public opinion/seize power, describes and comprehends an entire process: preparing for and then waging the armed struggle for power. And even during the period where creating public opinion is the main activity, there are elements, seeds of seizing power within the overall political preparation, that must be nurtured and developed. There must not only be the general understanding that the two aspects mutually interpenetrate with and influence each other, nor even just the understanding that at some point these aspects will change position, so that seizing power becomes principal, but also the ability to grasp when the basis for this shift is emerging — which may and very likely will happen suddenly and unexpectedly.

At the same time it must be understood that we are not just looking or waiting for a spontaneous uprising. In fact, under certain conditions, we might even try to *restrain* a spontaneous uprising. But this would only be correct if this was done on the basis of, and with the realistic practical possibility of, having a better shot at a more fully organized and coordinated insurrection in the *near future.* As opposed to 1905, the situation of the Bolsheviks in 1917 after the toppling of the Tsar — in particular the Bolsheviks' strengthened ties and influence among the class-conscious proletariat — did lead them to restrain premature attempts and spontaneous outbreaks of armed struggle between February and October 1917. But this was precisely on the basis of systematic work to fully bring to a head the contradictions that were leading toward a new revolutionary uprising, and the Bolsheviks did, as everyone knows, carry this through and strike when things were as ripe as they were going to get (though it took fierce struggle by Lenin to get the Bolshevik leadership to actually do so).

The point is not that the armed insurrection in the U.S. will be like 1917 or 1905 in Russia: undoubtedly in many important ways it will be like neither and will involve many new and unforeseen aspects — as is the case with all wars, revolutionary wars not least of all. The point is that we have to carry out our work to prepare ourselves, the advanced, and the broader masses as they awaken to political life, for different eventualities, and in particular different "sparks" that set off the armed struggle. While we must learn from historical experience, we must not be bound by stereotypes or search for "perfect models" or "ready-made revolutions." As Mao put it: "One must not be restricted. Lenin refused to be restricted by Marx. . . . One must not be superstitious. One must not be restricted. One must have new interpretations, new viewpoints, and creativity."[100]

[100] Mao, "Talk at Enlarged Meeting of the Political Bureau," *Miscellany*, Part II, p. 380.

I will conclude this first major part of this book with the following essential points in summary:

(1) Revolution is necessary to change the basic conditions in this society and the world and the basic direction of things. It is necessary to eliminate the *cause* of what does make life unlivable — already today for a great, great part of the people of the world, and potentially and quite literally for the overwhelming part of humanity itself.

(2) Revolution, including civil war with the inevitable disruption and destruction involved in that, is infinitely preferable to continued life under this system for the great majority of the world's people — and infinitely preferable, to all but the imperialists and their solid social base, to the "solution," the *only* "solution," they can provide.

(3) Revolutionary struggle in the world is inevitable and armed insurrection and civil war in the U.S. itself is both a possibility and under the right conditions is *winnable* for the proletariat. The advanced forces of revolution can have a significant bearing on this; our party's line and program provides the orientation, strategy, means, and methods for maximizing this possibility and the gains that can be made for the international proletariat and through it for humanity as a whole. Those who grasp what is involved and at stake must unite with and join the party and help push forward the carrying out of its central task — create public opinion/seize power — and its contribution to the world revolutionary struggle of the international proletariat.

II.

The Final Goal:

Looking Further at the Question Mao Raised Around the Novel *Water Margin*, or Settling for Nothing Less Than the Whole World and Its Complete Transformation

A General Introductory Explanation

Water Margin is a classical Chinese novel. Many in China have upheld it as "an immortal epic of peasant revolution."[101] But in 1975, in the course of his last great battle against revisionist betrayal — in particular against Deng Xiaoping and others who seized power after Mao's death and have taken China back down the road of capitalism and capitulation to imperialism — Mao focused attention on the real lesson of *Water Margin*. "The merit of the book *Water Margin*," Mao said then, "lies precisely in the portrayal of capitulation. It serves as teaching material by negative example to help all the people recognize capitulationists."[102] And he added: "*Water Margin* is against corrupt officials only, but not against the emperor." As Raymond Lotta explained in *And Mao Makes 5*, "Sung Chiang, who is the main figure in the novel, sneaks his way into the ranks of the peasant rebels and seizes leadership. After having put up a show of resistance for a while he capitulates to the emperor and turns on the peasant rebels."[103] (Sung Chiang is similar to the hero in medieval English tales, Robin Hood, who is cheated out of his rightful place in the nobility and becomes an outlaw, but fights only against the corrupt Prince John and only to restore the rightful ruler, Richard, to the throne and restore Robin's own

[101] "Unfold Criticism of 'Water Margin,'" *Peking Review* No. 37 (September 12, 1975), reprinted in *And Mao Makes 5*, edited with an introduction by Raymond Lotta (Chicago: Banner Press, 1978), p. 242.

[102] "Unfold Criticism of 'Water Margin,'" Lotta, ed., *And Mao Makes 5*, p. 241.

[103] Lotta, ed., *And Mao Makes 5*, Introduction, p. 32.

lost lands, wealth, and position in the realm. Another example of basically the same kind of thing is the relation of the Christians to the Roman Empire: from resistance to the elevation of Christianity as the enshrined state religion beginning with the reign of the Emperor Constantine.)

Such people are not thoroughgoing revolutionaries; they never break with the whole framework of the established order, and their orientation remains one of getting their fair share (or all they can) within that framework: if they fight against the powers-that-be, such fighting serves the purpose of striking a better deal with them at some point. And when that point comes, the whole logic of their outlook and objectives leads them not just to desert the revolutionary ranks but to become vicious opponents of revolution and to enlist themselves in a crusade against it. History has witnessed more than a few such people.

It is not necessarily the case that such people intended to follow this course all along, from the time they joined the revolutionary ranks, though that is definitely the case sometimes. There are many like the character Ah Q, created by the great Chinese revolutionary writer Lu Hsun, about whom Mao commented: "Actually, all Ah Q understands by revolution is helping himself to a few things just like some others."[104] The essential point is that unless people who rebel do make a leap to thoroughgoing opposition to the whole system and its ideology, ways of thinking, and values, they are liable to end up serving that same system, against revolution.

[104] Mao, "On the Ten Major Relationships," *MSW*, Vol. 5, p. 301. Another example that I'm reminded of is something that I saw years, more than 10 years ago now, back in the "mad years" of the late '60s, early '70s. One day someone handed me a public but not widely circulated manifesto from a group calling itself the Chicano Liberation Army in California. This manifesto listed all the various acts of guerrilla warfare they were going to carry out and so on and so forth in rather graphic detail, with indictments of the system — and some of these indictments were well-founded and you had to have basic agreement on that. But after doing all this they then summed it all up by expressing their determination to fight until "liberation is won. . .or until sufficient reforms are granted to redress our grievances." (I'm paraphrasing from memory here but that's the thrust of it.) This is the most classical and essentially explicit statement of "Sung Chiang-ism" that I at least can remember seeing in quite some time, although there are many contenders for that.

In returning to the question Mao raised around the novel *Water Margin*, I want to deal with its broader application and implications for revolution: the problem of making thoroughgoing revolution and sticking to it — and not just any kind of revolution but the communist revolution which involves, as Marx and Engels proclaimed, "the most radical rupture with traditional property relations; no wonder that its development involves the most radical rupture with traditional ideas."[105]

Proletarian Revolution Versus Bourgeois Revolution

The historical experience of proletarian revolution so far is that in general such revolutions have involved a significant bourgeois-democratic aspect and have actually passed through a bourgeois-democratic stage, whether shorter or more protracted. And it has proved to be much more difficult than anticipated to make the leap — or rupture — beyond bourgeois democracy to the socialist revolution, as a transitional stage and part of the overall world struggle for communism. The two great proletarian revolutions in history up to this point, the Russian and Chinese, each in their own way illustrate this.

The Chinese Revolution involved, as a necessary preparation for socialism, a bourgeois-democratic revolution — though one of a new type, led by the proletariat through its party and thus termed New Democracy by Mao. And as it turned out, this stage of the revolution involved a several decades-long struggle, itself passing through a complex process and several substages (most notably that of the War of Resistance against Japan). This new-democratic revolution was in its political and economic content anti-imperialist and antifeudal but not anticapitalist as such (although, as Mao pointed out, by striking at bureaucrat capital, which controlled 80 percent of industry, during this

[105] Karl Marx and Frederick Engels, *Manifesto of the Communist Party* (Peking: Foreign Languages Press, 1973), p. 59.

stage of the revolution a big blow was struck in undermining the foundations of capitalism in China, and in this respect there was an anticapitalist aspect to the new-democratic stage of the revolution).[106]

During this stage of the revolution, Mao wrote that this "new type of democratic revolution clears the way for capitalism on the one hand and creates the prerequisites for socialism on the other."[107] At that time and into the early years of the socialist stage after the founding of the People's Republic of China in 1949, this contradiction found expression mainly in terms of bourgeois forces outside the party more or less openly advocating capitalism and opposing socialism. But the more the socialist transformation of society advanced and the deeper it went in the following years, the more the main focus of this struggle changed to the fight against those within the Chinese Communist Party itself, especially at its top levels, who sought to take China down the capitalist road with themselves as the new, ruling bourgeoisie. In a sense this has proved to be, from an historical standpoint, the more profound expression of the fact that the new-democratic revolution cleared the way for two roads: the socialist road and the capitalist road (though, in the concrete circumstances of China in the world today, the capitalist road means capitalism subordinated to international capital, imperialism, as indeed has been the case since the capitalist-roaders seized power in China right after Mao's death in 1976).

Already in 1964, in discussing the tasks and content of the new-democratic revolution, Mao made the following very provocative remarks:

> New Democracy is a bourgeois-democratic revolution under the leadership of the proletariat. It touches only the landlords and the comprador bourgeoisie, it does not touch

[106] See Mao, *A Critique of Soviet Economics*, p. 40.

[107] Mao, "The Chinese Revolution and the Chinese Communist Party," *MSW*, Vol. 2, p. 327.

> the national bourgeoisie at all. To divide up the land and give it to the peasants is to transform the property of the feudal landlords into the individual property of the peasants, and this still remains within the limits of the bourgeois revolution. To divide up the land is nothing remarkable — MacArthur did it in Japan. Napoleon divided up the land too. Land reform cannot abolish capitalism, nor can it lead to socialism [i.e., in itself it does not constitute or achieve socialism — *B.A.*].[108]

A decade later, carrying this analysis further and deeper in his last great battle against Deng Xiaoping, et al., Mao summed up:

> With the socialist revolution they themselves come under fire. At the time of the cooperative transformation of agriculture there were people in the Party who opposed it, and when it comes to criticizing bourgeois right, they resent it. You are making the socialist revolution, and yet don't know where the bourgeoisie is. It is right in the Communist Party — those in power taking the capitalist road. The capitalist-roaders are still on the capitalist road.[109]

As Mao also summed up at that time, such people never make the leap beyond the bounds of bourgeois democracy — they never cross the narrow horizon of bourgeois right, to use Marx's phrase — and as the revolution reaches the socialist stage and continues and deepens in that stage, such people go from being bourgeois democrats to becoming capitalist-roaders — in the name of socialism and communism.

I pointed out in a paper submitted to our Central Committee in 1978 that for such people "socialism" means in essence the opportunity for them to lead their country — and themselves — to the status of an industrially developed, modernized nation, free from foreign domination and backwardness, and able to en-

[108] Mao, "Talk on Questions of Philosophy (August 18, 1964)," Schram, ed., *Chairman Mao Talks to the People*, p. 216.

[109] Cited in Fang Kang, "Capitalist-Roaders Are the Bourgeoisie Inside the Party," *Peking Review*, No. 25 (June 18, 1976), reprinted in Lotta, ed., *And Mao Makes 5*, p. 358.

joy the benefits and privileges that accompany this — especially for the ruling class.[110] (That such people may be unable to realize their grand designs is an historical irony but does not change the fact that this is the essence of their outlook and intent and the limit of their vision.) As a result of the revisionist coup in China an important negative lesson has been more profoundly provided, even if at a very bitter cost: now we do know much more clearly "where the bourgeoisie is" under socialism. But beyond this heightened recognition, as important as it is, what is fundamental to grasp is the underlying material and historical basis for this — and for the struggle against it. This resides not just in the nature of socialist society as a transition between capitalism and communism but in the world contradictions of this, the era of imperialism and the proletarian revolution, and the major expressions these contradictions assume in any given period, and especially at key turning points in world history such as the present.

Although Russia at the time of the October Revolution of 1917 was an imperialist country, it was a backward one which in certain respects was "imperialized" by other, more developed and powerful imperialisms (in particular British and French imperialism). In important ways, not only geographically but economically and politically, Russia was a kind of bridge between West and East. In the development of the Russian Revolution there was a bourgeois-democratic stage and even after Lenin summed up (following the February 1917 Revolution that toppled the Tsar) that the situation had changed and the socialist revolution had come on the agenda as the immediate stage, he also recognized the fact that there remained many bourgeois-democratic questions that were as yet unresolved with the triumph of the October Revolution. Besides the task of ending national oppression — and very much bound up with this as an underlying condition — was the land/peasant question, which remained an essential problem in building socialism

[110] *Thoughts on Points for Discussion*, an unpublished paper submitted by Bob Avakian to the Central Committee of the RCP,USA and adopted by it in 1978.

in the Soviet Union over the next several decades. In fact, this problem proved to be extremely difficult to handle, and this difficulty was very much a factor in the undermining and eventual overthrowing of socialism in the Soviet Union (though not in the mechanical materialist, "one-to-one" sense that it is impossible to build socialism in a backward, largely peasant country, as is claimed by various Trotskyites, social democrats, and other pseudorevolutionaries and pseudosocialists with dead souls).

It is important to note in this connection that on the one hand, in summing up the problems and errors in the Soviet Union and the causes for the triumph of revisionism there (beginning with the coming to power of a new bourgeoisie headed by Khrushchev in the mid-1950s), Mao focused a great deal on the problems and errors in dealing with the peasantry (for example in his 1956 speech "On the Ten Major Relationships" and in his reading notes on a Soviet political economy textbook in the early '60s).[111] On the other hand, however, perhaps he didn't link this enough (or deeply enough) with the question of whether or not and to what degree bourgeois-democratic tasks and problems actually remained unresolved throughout the almost four decades of socialism in the USSR. For example, he says, "The October Revolution was a socialist revolution which concomitantly fulfilled tasks left over from the bourgeois democratic revolution."[112] This analysis may seem correct on the surface; however a deeper summation suggests that neither "concomitantly" (i.e., as an accompaniment) nor "fulfilled" is altogether correct. Perhaps more than Mao recognized, efforts to carry out such tasks — in particular, in regard to the land/peasant question — involved intense contradiction which had a great deal to do with the strengthening of bourgeois forces in Soviet society — including within the party itself — and the

[111] See Mao, "On the Ten Major Relationships," *MSW*, Vol. 5, pp. 284-307, especially pp. 289-92; and Mao, *A Critique of Soviet Economics*.

[112] Mao, *Critique of Soviet Economics*, p. 39. Another translation of this I have seen reads "incidentally accomplished," but in any case the essential point is the same. See Mao, "Reading Notes on the Soviet Union's 'Political Economics' (1961-1962)," *Miscellany*, Part II, p. 251.

eventual triumph of revisionism.[113]

These kinds of problems are likely to be with us for some time. This is very much linked with the phenomenon of lopsidedness in the world and with the political and ideological distortions that tend to accompany it. As I pointed out in *For a Harvest of Dragons*, corresponding to this lopsidedness,

> in the sphere of politics and ideology, and within the Marxist movement in particular (broadly defined), has been the marked tendency (of avowed Marxists) toward social-democracy in the imperialist countries and toward nationalism in the oppressed nations (though the latter has the virtue of often assuming a revolutionary expression, even if not a thoroughly Marxist-Leninist one).[114]

In other words, there remains a strong material basis in the world today for the pull of bourgeois ideology, in one form or another. And, if there is world war/nuclear devastation, in such circumstances the problems of this kind — of people continuing to view things, even the struggle against the established order (or the attempt to reimpose that order), through the prism of bourgeois ideology, even in terms of "what do I get out of it" (like Lu Hsun's character Ah Q) — will hardly be made less acute!

All this stresses the crucial necessity, especially for the vanguard and the advanced but also the oppressed masses more broadly, to grasp the profound, fundamental difference between proletarian revolution and bourgeois democracy — even bourgeois-democratic *revolution.* This means confronting the question of making the "two radical ruptures" Marx and Engels spoke of in the *Communist Manifesto* and grasping that this problem can only be attacked at its roots, let alone solved, with a firm internationalist approach and through liberating and

[113] Here I have only briefly noted, in the most general terms, some basic questions and underlying problems; these points are addressed in more detail in *Conquer the World* (see Part I, "Further Historical Perspectives on the First Advances in Seizing and Exercising Power — Proletarian Dictatorship — and Embarking on the Socialist Road," pp. 1-36, especially pp. 19-22), but still more thorough, all-around summation of this needs to be made.

[114] Avakian, *For a Harvest of Dragons*, p. 145.

transforming the whole world — and as much of it as possible at each stage.

QUESTIONS RELATING TO THE EXPERIENCE AND LESSONS OF THE '60s MOVEMENT IN THE U.S.

"We tried that before."... You tried *what*?

As important and radical in many ways as the '60s movement in the U.S. was — especially the more revolutionary currents that developed — there still was not, even on the part of the most influential revolutionary forces, that radical rupture with (leap beyond) the confines of bourgeois democracy, in particular patriotism (nationalism) in one form or another and the thrust of fighting for "equality" as the essential and highest goal. Such a goal (as I argued in the pamphlet *Bob Avakian Replies to a Letter From "Black Nationalist With Communistic Inclinations"*), "as a general category,... is itself a phenomenon of the bourgeois epoch" and ultimately remains within the confines of bourgeois democracy.[115]

More fundamentally, in the U.S. in the '60s there was of course no radical rupture with the underlying property relations — in short, no revolutionary overthrow of imperialism to undertake the transformation of economic and social relations as well as politics and ideology. That is precisely what remains — and cries out ever more urgently — to be done.

In "Cynicism and the Shift in World Relations" I pointed out that the increase of such cynicism in the U.S. (and other countries) these days "is very much related to the shift in world relations that has occurred since the 1960s, and in particular the shift in the principal contradiction in the world from that be-

[115] *Bob Avakian Replies to a Letter From "Black Nationalist With Communistic Inclinations"* (Chicago: RCP Publications, 1981), p. 6.

tween the oppressed nations and imperialism to what is the principal contradiction today: the contradiction among the imperialists themselves and specifically between the two imperialist blocs," so that the main — certainly not the only but the main — conflict in the world today is between two sets of oppressors, two bulwarks of reaction. And "it is not hard to see how this could spread confusion and even feed cynicism."[116] On the other hand, particularly in the case of those who have made an article of faith, a way of life — and even capital — out of such cynicism, there is no justification at all, and it must be said that this is the most facile, cheap cop-out (anybody can do it!). And worst of all is that "worldly wise" cynicism that acts as if those of us who haven't learned not to hate oppression and haven't capitulated just haven't "woken up and smelled the coffee," haven't "come to terms" with the "real world," as if the present world — that is, its dominant relations, values, and ideologies, and all their attendant evils — is the only possible reality, as if people *ought* to "come to terms" with it. . . or as if it has all that much prospect of remaining permanent anyway! (Do these people know how really *old* they have become?)

If you weren't trying for revolution but for reform "in your youth," then don't act like somebody betrayed you because things are still the same and worse and everything that revolted you and caused you to revolt is still there, and getting more pronounced all the time. If you were trying for revolution but became discouraged, it's important to grasp two basic facts:

(1) There were many limitations to what even we revolutionaries (including certainly the Revolutionary Union at that time) were fighting for and how we were fighting — how we saw and presented revolution itself (again the question of "the tenor of the times" and the character of the movements, even the most revolutionary, in the U.S. in the '60s and the question of a radical rupture, or the lack of it, as mentioned earlier).

(2) Naturally things are worse: they still run U.S. society

[116] See "Provocations," *RW*, No. 228, p. 3.

and dominate the world.[117] The point is that *our work is unfinished*: to make revolution — *proletarian* revolution as part of the world revolutionary struggle of the international proletariat. And the task before us is clearer, its necessity more sharply expressed, than in the '60s. Some painful but invaluable lessons have been learned.

The Struggle of Black People, Bourgeois Democracy and Proletarian Revolution

The '60s movement among Black people was the most advanced revolutionary expression of that period in the U.S. — and it was the most advanced revolutionary mass movement that has yet erupted in the U.S., not only in terms of militant resistance and rebellion but especially in terms of its basic alienation from and opposition to the whole social order and in its identification with the enemies of America (U.S. imperialism) particularly in the Third World. On the other hand, even this most revolutionary expression did not make a thorough rupture with bourgeois democracy.

There is of course a bourgeois-democratic aspect to the struggle of Black people against their oppression (including their right, as a nation, to self-determination), and it is a damning indictment of the imperialist system that it cannot bring about the equality of nations and must in fact foster and reinforce national oppression. But first of all, as the experience of the '60s in the U.S. — and historical and international experience generally — has shown, there can be no thoroughgoing struggle against

[117] Here I'm reminded of a comment by Lawrence Kasdan, director of *The Big Chill*. Apparently he said in an interview that he and many others like him — and like the characters in that movie, whom he sees as being more or less expressive, collectively, of his own experiences and views — thought for a while, as a result of the '60s, that they had a major if not a determining voice in regard to what kind of society the U.S. would be and what its relations would be with the rest of the world. These, of course, are the illusions of reformists, but they have infected many revolutionaries or erstwhile revolutionaries as well; the awakening has been rude indeed and, not surprisingly, disorienting and demoralizing.

imperialism and no complete shattering of the bonds of national oppression without the leadership of a proletarian, as opposed to a bourgeois-democratic, line and program. Further and more fundamental, there remains the fact that equality as such falls ultimately within the framework of bourgeois democracy, that it cannot solve or even fundamentally address class division, exploitation and oppression, and the whole dog-eat-dog relations and mentality characteristic of the present system. Therefore, ironically, an orientation based on equality as the essential goal cannot even fully and finally bring about the abolition of social inequality.

To examine this more concretely in terms of the experience and lessons of the '60s, it is helpful to focus on Malcolm X and the Black Panther Party — the person and the organization that most represented the revolutionary current among Black people and within the '60s movements in general in the U.S.[118]

On Malcolm X

Overwhelmingly the main thing about Malcolm X, which made him stand out from every other major Black leader of his time (the early '60s), was his basic revolutionary stand: his defiance right in the face of the system; his uncompromising hatred for the oppression of the Black masses and his determination to fight against it; his bold disloyalty to America and exposure of its whole history of barbarous crimes against Black people and others — Malcolm X called them out for what they are in a way few had before — and especially after his break with the Nation of Islam ("Black Muslims") of Elijah Muhammed, his increasing efforts to link up with other struggles, particularly in the Third

[118] Here it is important to recall, however, that "the '60s" was not one uniform period and "the '60s movement" was not one uniform political tendency. They were characterized by sharply contradictory trends and specifically within "the movement" there was both a reformist and a revolutionary trend, the former generally dominant in the first part of the '60s, the latter if not dominant had at least considerable initiative in the late '60s and in many ways put reformism on the defensive then.

World, against American imperialism. It is for this reason that Malcolm X is remembered, respected, and loved by millions of Black people, and other oppressed people, not only in the U.S. but internationally, and why the revolutionary proletariat upholds him as a great fighter against imperialism.

On the other hand and secondarily, Malcolm X, as a revolutionary but a revolutionary nationalist (or "Black nationalist freedom fighter," in his words), did not (or had not by the time he was cut down by agents of imperialism in 1965) ultimately cross beyond the narrow horizon of bourgeois right, to utilize Marx's phrase. Not only was his battle against the oppression of Black people still limited by the confines of (and couched in general in terms of) equality,[119] but his practical program as far as he had developed it, even after leaving the Nation of Islam, retained a strong strain of Black capitalism.

This comes through clearly — along with the main thing: his scathing indictment of American imperialism and his identification with those, especially the Vietnamese people, waging struggle against it — in one of his last major speeches, *The Ballot or the Bullet* (1964). As the title suggests, in this speech Malcolm argued that it was still possible — though time was running out he said — for America to have a "bloodless revolution" by giving "the Black man in this country everything that is due him — everything!" He also advocated the tactics of uniting the Black vote as a powerful bloc to punish enemies and reward friends and force the granting of justice to Black people. It is not without significance that a variation of this tactic can be advocated and applied today — though with very different objectives and intentions — by a counterrevolutionary lackey of imperialism, Jesse Jackson. At best, as with Malcolm, this tactic assumes, wrongly, that votes convey real political power, and further that the differences within the ruling class are greater

[119] This basic stand for equality was not applied, however, to women. Malcolm never really broke with a backward, patriarchal position on this question. Weaknesses on the woman question, in various forms, were a general problem with the movements of the '60s — about which more shortly.

than their common antagonism with the oppressed. Such a tactic ignores or denies that political power has a class character, that there is a state apparatus serving one class in suppressing another, and at bottom that this state reflects and serves a certain division of labor in society and an economic system with its dynamic motion and "logic" — which sets the terms for politics and dictates that certain class interests dominate, whichever group of individuals is in office.

And in *The Ballot or the Bullet* Malcolm also advocates promoting and supporting Black businesses — (just as the white man supports and patronizes white businesses) as the solution to the economic exploitation of Black people — a program which has been attempted before and since by Black petty-bourgeois and aspiring bourgeois elements but which has not ended — and cannot end — the exploitation of the masses of Black people (nor even completely eliminate the discrimination faced by the Black petty bourgeoisie and bourgeoisie for that matter).

Of course, as already stated, these things were not the main thrust of this speech or of Malcolm's stand overall (Malcolm makes clear that he thinks such a "peaceful revolution" extremely unlikely — a chicken never gave birth to a duck egg, and if it did it would be a revolutionary chicken, is how he put it in another speech). But the contradiction between reform and revolution, as symbolized by the title, *The Ballot or the Bullet*, runs through this speech and through Malcolm's position overall, though revolution not reform was clearly the main aspect and leading edge.

Today, with the changes in the U.S. and the world as a whole, including the fostering of elite strata among Black people and their special service to U.S. imperialism in promoting the line among Black people that they have — or must have — a stake in this system and should fight to defend it so they can get their share — in these circumstances, it is ironic but not unexplainable that such people echo or parallel parts of what was

Malcolm's program in the '60s.[120] The point is definitely not that Malcolm himself was an upholder rather than a staunch opponent of this system (they didn't shoot him down for nothing, after all!) but that programs and strategies that do not represent a full rupture with the imperialist system and its ideology cannot sustain a consistent all-the-way-to-the-end struggle against it and under certain circumstances can and will be taken over and used by that very system and those who conciliate with it. What this spotlights once again is the crucial importance, especially with today's world situation and the stakes it holds, for those who hate and rebel against this system to make that radical rupture — that leap beyond the bourgeois-democratic framework to the only thoroughly revolutionary position, that of the revolutionary proletariat.

More on the Black Panther Party

Here my purpose is not to repeat the analysis I made in *Summing Up the Black Panther Party* but to add to and hopefully deepen that analysis, specifically in terms of the errors, weaknesses, and limitations in the Black Panther Party's own outlook and program that contributed — in the face of murderous repression by the state — to the demise of the Black Panther Party as a revolutionary organization. In going into this, however, it is necessary to repeat what was said at the very beginning of that pamphlet:

> First of all, now that the Black Panther Party no longer exists as a revolutionary organization and barely exists at all, except as a pitiful reformist and petty gangster sect, it is tempting to discard, to negate and to wipe out all its tremen-

[120] It is even possible to find this in a communist guise — the combination of Black nationalism, painted pink with lots of workerist posturing, as well as good old American chauvinism — for one example check out the "works" of Amiri Baraka in recent years.

> dous achievements and all that it contributed to this decisive, earthshaking period of the 1960s and early 1970s and the development toward revolution in this country. But that is a great mistake. . . .
>
> You see, the Black Panther Party in this country, despite weaknesses in its understanding and political program, turned thousands, even tens of thousands, perhaps even hundreds of thousands of people toward revolution in this country. Thousands and thousands of young people in particular — Black, white, Chicano, Puerto Rican and others — were turned toward revolution and even some toward Marxism by the work, by the political activity, and by the propaganda and the agitation carried out by the Black Panther Party. . . .
>
> . . . We have to understand what the contributions of people like that were and why they were finally turned around, so the same thing doesn't happen again.[121]

In that pamphlet I focused on two main errors of the Black Panther Party: first its attempt to "combine a little bit of internationalism and a little bit of nationalism" and "even more fundamental . . . the main disease that has plagued the communist movement in this country, the old Communist Party and the revolutionary movement going back a long way, and that disease is pragmatism. . . . And what pragmatism says is basically this: just rely on what's immediately before you, whatever your direct and immediate experience tells you is true or good, that's all you need to know, don't ask the question why, don't try to discover what's going on with it, don't try to see it in its relationship with anything else, just accept it and do it."[122] Carrying forward with this analysis, specifically in terms of pragmatism, it is important to look at a statement by Huey P. Newton, founder and leader of the Black Panther Party: "Power," he said, "is the ability to define phenomena and cause them to act in the desired manner." This was not just an isolated statement but was fundamental to the

[121] Bob Avakian, *Summing Up the Black Panther Party* (Chicago: RCP Publications, 1979), pp. 1-2.

[122] Avakian, *Summing Up the Black Panther Party*, pp. 5, 7.

outlook and line of the Black Panther Party, and to its errors.

Well, what is wrong with this statement? At bottom it represents a view that there is no objective reality, independent of anyone's (or everyone's) wishes, wills, perceptions — or powers. To say that power is the ability to define phenomena is really to say that the phenomena don't have an existence and particular character (a "definition") of their own and can be made to be anything that anyone — or more specifically those with the most power in any given situation — wants or wills them to be. This is itself a profoundly pragmatic view, idealist at base (denying the existence of objective reality independent of ideas or wills, reversing the correct relationship, as if ideas or wills are what give rise to or determine the nature of objective reality, as if that reality is an extension or projection of ideas, wills, etc.).

In fact, the ideas, wills, actions, and so on of people can and do greatly affect and change reality, but they do not and cannot make things (phenomena) whatever they want them to be, just by "defining" them. If I define a poisonous toadstool as a harmless (and delicious) mushroom, that does not make it any less poisonous (nor does defining a rabid animal as a harmless house pet make it so); and if I define a bourgeois dictatorship as a democracy with no class character, that does not make the repressive apparatus of the bourgeois state any less real or repressive. And so on. Power does not lie in "defining" these phenomena as I might like to but in grasping their essence — which means their internal contradictions and motion and change as well — and their relation to other things, and on *that* basis dealing with and changing them. This can only be done in the fullest sense through the application of a comprehensive, all-around view of reality and the principles involved in its development — which is the science of Marxism-Leninism-Mao Tsetung Thought.

Finally, Huey Newton's definition of power expresses a narrow conception of what the essence and purpose of power — in particular political power — is. In class society (and outside class society the concept of political power has no real meaning since it implies the power of one section of society over another) political power means that a particular class dominates and shapes the political institutions and that its ideas and values are the ruling ones in society. This is based, however, on a certain *material foundation*: the level of development of the productive forces (technology and the people with the knowledge and ability to use and develop it) and the relations people enter into to utilize those productive forces at a given stage. And when the domination by a particular class of the superstructure (politics and ideology) no longer corresponds to that material foundation — which in turn means that the production relations among the people no longer correspond to but act as a fetter on the development of the productive forces — then sooner or later there will be a revolution to overthrow the existing political power and establish new economic and social relations and a corresponding superstructure.

Without grasping this fundamental truth revealed by Marxism, the question of power (political power in particular) could only be viewed as an arbitrary thing — whoever somehow grabs it would be able to hang on to it indefinitely, unless they were stupid or someone simply more "powerful" came along; struggles in society would be, as the bourgeoisie never tires of saying they are, the so-called "survival of the fittest," with fittest being the most cunning and ruthless. But there have been many ruling classes in history that have been cunning and ruthless — perhaps even more so than those who rose up against them — yet they have been overthrown anyway, because of the very ways in which society does develop, as summarized here. Further, the view that "power is the ability to define phenomena and cause them to act in the desired manner" also makes it a subjective question: just what is "a desired manner" depends on an individual or group's arbitrary will or wishes.

For all these reasons, this view is not one in accord with the actual development of society, including its most decisive development through revolutionary leaps from one form of society to another. In the final analysis this formulation by Huey P. Newton is not only an erroneous but a conservative view of the world and the struggle to change it, a view which ran counter to and undermined the revolutionary side, indeed the whole revolutionary thrust, of the Black Panther Party at the time of its founding and at the height of its influence in the late 1960s.

All this was connected with another major contradiction within the Black Panther Party, specifically in terms of its strategic orientation. Its strategy was, to put it that way, a combination of a confused strategy and no strategy. By this I mean, in part, that the Panthers attempted to develop a program to address the grievances of the Black masses, but they were never entirely clear on what the overall solution was to this — as well as to the overall oppression and exploitation and international marauding carried out by U.S. imperialism, which they also fought against. Did U.S. imperialism have to be overthrown, or could Black people (and other oppressed people) win liberation without this? If revolution was necessary, *what kind* of revolution — with what aims and programs, achieved through what strategy and what means? Were the Panthers in favor of a struggle to win a separate state for Black people? Or should Black people take part in a larger revolution to change U.S. society as a whole? Or some combination of these two things? The Black Panther Party grappled with these kinds of basic questions but never clearly, definitively determined where it stood on them or on a number of other questions of great importance for the revolutionary movement internationally (such as the struggle against Soviet revisionism).

The Black Panther Party increasingly found itself in the worst of both worlds. It took a basic revolutionary stand, but had no clear vision, program, or strategy for revolution. It reached out for broader coalitions, but had no clear-cut analysis of the class forces that had to be allied with or opposed and defeated to make revolution. It stood up to the state and other armed reactionaries in armed struggle but had no overall strategic orientation for how to carry out the overthrow of the state and for handling the relationship at different points between armed struggle and overall political struggle and political work.

All this is linked not only with the Black Panther Party's

underlying pragmatism but also with its attempts "to combine a little bit of internationalism and a little bit of nationalism." And in an overall way it is very much linked with the question of rupturing — or in the case of the Black Panther Party *not* making a thoroughgoing rupture in the final analysis — with bourgeois democracy, with the "narrow horizon of bourgeois right" and therefore with the orientation of fighting to ultimately come to terms with and find your place — your "fair" or "equal" share — within the present order and scheme of things (like Sung Chiang in the novel *Water Margin*).

The point, again, is not to deny the many and truly great contributions of the Black Panther Party to the revolutionary movement, nor certainly to argue that they lacked the desire to make revolution. As I said in *Summing Up the Black Panther Party*, "It wasn't because they lacked the courage or determination or a burning desire to rise up and overthrow this system that the Panther Party backed off, that many of its leaders — those who weren't killed — sold out. It was because their understanding was not thoroughgoing enough. . . . So despite the revolutionary heroism and determination and the many great contributions of the Panther Party they more and more turned away from revolution toward reform"[123] — or toward ill-fated adventurism that at bottom also rejected thoroughgoing revolution and sought a "shortcut" to the desired change.

In many crucial ways we today are building on the achievements of the Black Panther Party. The fact that it contributed so much and yet still was not able to continue forward as a revolutionary organization is not a reason for us to fall into despair but is all the more reason why it is crucial to thoroughly and penetratingly sum up the errors and limitations of the Panthers while continuing to uphold and popularize their heroic stands and revolutionary daring, their many correct insights into the problems of making revolution in a country such as the U.S., and the many ways in which for a few sweet years they made reformism jump back.

[123] Avakian, *Summing Up the Black Panther Party*, pp. 15, 9.

As Mao Said, "Historical Experience Merits Attention"

A profound lesson can be drawn from the whole bloodthirsty history of Zionism and the state of Israel on where one will be led with the outlook of "anything is justified for my people to get ahead (with qualified people like me in the lead) given how much we have suffered throughout history." This is a question for everyone fighting oppression — including those who might be called "Black Zionists" — to ponder.

Disorientation from Failure — and from "Success"

There is, especially among Black people but also among the basic masses (and others) more generally, a certain disorientation and in some cases even conservatism right now, not only because (as it is often put) the struggle of the '60s did not succeed or accomplish anything real, but because in another way it *did* achieve something, including some of the things that were being aimed for in that period. There are today, in a way there were not 15-20 years ago, many Black elected officials, a fair number of Black people in the media, etc., and there has been a building up of some Black business (and this continues today, despite the fact that some are being allowed, or even pushed in some cases, to go under). The focus on this is "the '60s" that bourgeois elements and lackeys among Black people and other oppressed peoples in the U.S. want to "replay" — and in the present situation this can only be a retrograde trend, especially to the extent (and it *is* to a large extent the case) that this is a conscious attempt to negate the revolutionary currents of the late '60s and a conscious effort to lead the oppressed masses more firmly into the deadly embrace of the imperialist ruling class.

It is of course not the case that basic equality has been won for Black people and other oppressed peoples in the U.S. But certain things have changed and certain things have been gained, in particular for the more privileged and elite strata among them, and especially in today's "hard times" and with the approaching showdown with the Soviet bloc, a significant mood exists among these strata of scuffling to preserve what they have got, including by "going along with the program" of the U.S. imperialists. Further, even among those who have not benefited from the concessions and co-optations by the ruling class and whose situation has grown worse since the '60s, there is significant disorientation: not just disorientation at the fact that after so much struggle things are worse — and this is the situation for the basic masses generally — but also to some degree the disorientation of not knowing exactly what should be struggled for after all, since many of the specific things demanded in the '60s *have* been granted, at least up to a point.

This is linked not only with the sharpened class polarization among Black people which we have been emphasizing,[124] but it is also another sharp illustration of the need for that radical rupture with the whole bourgeois-democratic framework — and on the other hand how crucial and liberating for the basic proletarian masses that rupture is. It is only as such a rupture is made that the fundamental class interests of these proletarians and of the proletariat as a whole can be really fought for uncompromisingly (and as a vital part of this, that the oppression of Black people as a people, which does victimize them across class lines — though in significantly different ways and to different degrees for different classes — can be attacked at its roots).

The Woman Question and the "Two Radical Ruptures"

In many ways, and particularly for men, the woman question and whether you seek to completely abolish or to preserve the

[124] See, for example, Bob Avakian, "Class Polarization Among Black People," *RW*, No. 154 (May 7, 1982), p. 3.

existing property and social relations and corresponding ideology that enslave women (or maybe "just a little bit" of them) is a touchstone question *among the oppressed themselves.* It is a dividing line between "wanting in" and really "wanting out": between fighting to end all oppression and exploitation — and the very division of society into classes — and seeking in the final analysis to get your part in this, the difference between real revolutionaries and Ah Qs.[125]

Black Women

The suppressed position of Black women in the '60s movement of Black people (and this was true for women generally, but there were particular expressions of this concerning Black women that hold some valuable lessons, by negative example) and the rationalization for this are something which cannot go — and indeed have not gone — unchallenged. From straight-up bourgeois scholars to so-called revolutionaries (including some women, such as the impostor Angela Davis,[126] as well as many men), the notion has been propagated that inequality between women and men and the oppression of women by men does not exist or apply in the same way among Black people as among others — or even that it is reversed! This includes the idea (whether stated straight-up or slightly disguised) that the "emasculation of the Black man" has created a situation where it is necessary for him first to realize his "manhood," including by lording it over women, and then maybe the question of equality between the sexes can be taken up.

It is a truth and a searing indictment of America that Black men in the U.S. have suffered barbarous oppression — including literal emasculation — at the hands of slaveowners and

[125] In this regard see Bob Avakian, "We Want In . . . We Want Out — Opposite Views on Discrimination and Degradation," *RW*, No. 199 (April 1, 1983), p. 3.

[126] See, for example, Angela Davis, *Women, Race & Class* (New York: Vintage Books, 1983).

other white oppressors. But oppression has assumed forms no less barbarous with regard to Black women. And the answer to the centuries-long oppression of Black people, *women and men*, in the whole historical development and present-day reality of the U.S. (an oppression which has, however, had different features in different eras) is not to "restore the rites" of patriarchy. Patriarchy and "male rights" serve imperialism, the bourgeoisie, oppression, exploitation, and the division of society into classes and everything that goes with them: they will never serve the struggle to abolish these things.

Secondly, the oppression of Black people has never resulted and does not result today in a situation where Black women have a position of equality with — nor still less that they have a superior position to — Black men (or any other men). The fact is, Black women are oppressed — by Black men as well as more generally by men and most fundamentally by the whole system. (Of course individual cases where women have fucked over men can be cited among Black people as well as in general, and the same could also be said in terms of individual Black people fucking over individual white people, but we are talking about *basic social relations* here.) And the ending of these unequal and oppressive social relations between men and women is an integral and indispensable part of the overall struggle to end all oppression: the emancipation of the proletariat — and of mankind itself from the fetters and evils of class-divided society — is impossible without the emancipation of women. If you think being free means or must include having a woman (or more than one) to oppress, then you are still striving for the "freedom" of capitalism, not the emancipation of communism — you are still an Ah Q, not a proletarian revolutionary, you are only against corrupt officials, and not against the whole empire.

This question — the position and role of Black women and of women generally in society and in the struggle to transform it — will be a big question in the '80s, far beyond what it was in the '60s. This marks an important difference between the '60s and the '80s and reflects the fundamental differences in terms of what is on the historical agenda and what the stakes are: a far more extreme and radical solution is demanded and will be brought about — in one direction or another.[127]

The position of the masses of women, and in particular Black women, especially today — where roughly half the Black families with children under 18 are headed by women, to cite just one significant aspect of the overall situation — on the one hand involves a tremendous burden of oppression that weighs them down but on the other hand gives rise to a no less tremendous, even if often suppressed, outrage and a restless questioning and desire for some way out, for drastic change from conditions and from a whole world that becomes increasingly unbearable. This is the fury that must be unleashed as a mighty force for revolution — and there is a stronger basis for this today than at any time in the past.

It is not accidental that much of the resistance and political movements of opposition that are taking place today find women playing a major and in many cases initiating and leading role (the antiwar and antinuclear movements, not only in the U.S. but in other countries as well, being important examples), and that there is much militant resistance by women to their oppression. The imperialists have their reasons and needs for involving women in certain aspects of society from which they have been largely shut out (such as the military!), which has all to do with their preparations for world war. That *this* is why they would even allow or encourage some of the breaking down of barriers to women that has gone on, while at the same time they promote, through the various media and by other means, the most brutal and debasing oppression of women — from pornography to offensives in the realm of fashion to the Moral Majority's spearhead of restoring the "proper place" and role for women, as man's subordinate in the home and in society at large — this provides a vivid and grotesque exposure of their whole system

[127] This is reflected in some influential cultural works (novels, poems, and so on) that have been brought forward by women — with Black women a particular and significant part of this — in recent years, dealing not only with the woman question in various aspects but with other important social questions as well.

and why it is not worth a single drop of blood to defend — but many to overthrow.

Out of their own necessity, and despite their furious attempts to intensify the oppression and degradation of women and smother their outrage, the imperialists are raising up a terrible force whose basic interests — speaking of the vast majority of women — cannot help but be radically opposed to this whole system with its institutionalization of patriarchal right and its systematic oppression, suffocation, and mutilation of women, body and soul. How could most women *not* want a basic change in a society where a woman will be raped *every eight minutes* while the rulers of that society ravage people throughout the world and plot a war that could blow the world up to defend this way of life! To unite with and seek to fully unleash, or to fear, hate, and seek to suppress the fury of this terrible force: this is a *fundamental dividing line* and has a great deal to do with whether things in the '80s go qualitatively beyond the '60s on the revolutionary road.

OTHER IMPORTANT QUESTIONS RELATING TO THE QUESTION MAO RAISED AROUND THE NOVEL *WATER MARGIN*

Getting Left Behind in the '60s-'70s ('80s) Shift

In the article "The '60s-'70s Shift"[128] and a number of other places I have spoken to the phenomena of many forces, not only in the U.S. but internationally, who took a revolutionary stand in the '60s but have, with the shifting of world relations and world contradictions through the '70s and into the '80s, abandoned

[128] See "The '60s-'70s Shift," *RW*, No. 149 (April 2, 1982), p. 3.

revolution either openly or in the guise of embracing such things as the "realistic socialism" practiced in the Soviet Union and its bloc. With those articles as reference points (and without attempting to repeat the whole analysis made there), I want to speak to a few significant expressions of this.

First is the phenomenon of nationalists, including many who were revolutionary nationalists in the '60s, now embracing reformism, in particular in the form of social-democracy (reformist socialism based on bourgeois democracy) in addition to those who have embraced revisionism, of the Soviet variety most often. This has been of some significance in the U.S. but is an international phenomenon, including in the Third World, where a number of forces have put down the gun and picked up the ballot — have given up on the strategic orientation of armed revolution, including active all-around preparation for waging it when it is not immediately on the agenda.

Another phenomenon akin to this but taking a different or even an "opposite" form, is the tactic of using armed struggle as a lever and bargaining chip for striking some kind of deal with the established order rather than conducting armed struggle in such a way that it becomes a mass-based, all-the-way revolutionary struggle. This tactic (a classic example of "Sung Chiang-ism") has been employed by a whole menagerie of opportunists, from various sects in places like Lebanon to more Marxist groups identifying themselves to one degree or another with Soviet revisionist social-imperialism (socialism in words, imperialism in deeds). In the cases of the latter forces in particular, this tactic is often used as a companion to the tactics of "peaceful transition," with first one and then the other tactic employed (or the two coordinated simultaneously with a certain division of labor among their forces). But the "bottom line" remains using these forms of struggle, and any masses involved in them, as wedges and bargaining chips to alter the "balance of forces" more in line with the narrow interests of such forces and with the interests and requirements of Soviet social-imperialism to the degree possible, depending on the situation. All this is another factor complicating the situation and the tasks of the revolutionary communists, who must take these tactics into account and learn how to counter and defeat them and expose their fundamentally counterrevolutionary nature and purpose — bringing out in theory and as soon as possible in practice the fundamental difference between a revolutionary war of the masses and gun-toting, cutthroating revisionism.

Another serious problem: in today's world situation, clinging to analyses which were previously correct but no longer correctly reflect reality not only can lead to immobilization, but worse to landing in — or at least gravitating toward — the wrong camp. A sharp example of this: persisting in the analysis that the main contradiction in the world is between the oppressed nations (or the Third World) and imperialism — as was the case in the '60s but is no longer so because of the major changes that came about in the "'60s-'70s ('80s) shift" — will not only leave one unable to really grasp the dangers and opportunities imminently shaping up in the world; it will also propel you toward the Soviet Union sooner or later (and given the pace of world events, "later" may not mean all that much later) if you don't openly come into alliance with "classical" (Western) imperialism. This is for two main reasons:

(1) The U.S., not the Soviet Union, has the lion's share of colonies and the largest sphere of influence among the imperialists at this point; and

(2) The Soviet Union still has a socialist cover and as a major tactic makes use of it to pose as the "natural ally" of struggles in the Third World (and elsewhere) against U.S. imperialism and its allies and to utilize these struggles for its own imperialist ends.[129] The Soviet Union not only has a socialist cover, however. It also has real material force to oppose the considerable material force of the U.S. and its bloc — and where it suits their interests the Soviets make weaponry, technical assistance, etc., available in sufficient quantity and in such a way as to make the

[129] This raises the other side of the coin: those who oppose Soviet imperialism but don't at the same time take a clear-cut stand opposed to "classical" Western imperialism will, wittingly or unwittingly, willingly or unwillingly, act as ammunition for the latter in its international thuggery and rivalry with the Soviet bloc.

prospect of such "aid" attractive and to ensnare those who fall for the bait.

All this is something we have pointed to before (and there have been more than a few examples of anti-imperialist movements and organizations that have fallen into the clutches of the Soviet social-imperialists, especially with the '60s-'70s ('80s) shift — from which it is very important to draw appropriate lessons).[130] But this is also a battle that will have to be repeatedly waged. This not only means continuing exposure of and struggle against the Soviet social-imperialist bloc as well as U.S. imperialism and the Western imperialist bloc; it also means continuing and deepening analysis of and struggle over the character of the world situation today and its urgent prospects.

An Example of an "Emperor/Corrupt Officials" Shell Game

A favorite tactic of the imperialists these days, particularly the U.S. imperialists, is the tactic of letting others do the dirty work of murder and massacre while they stay in the background posing as the benevolent patriarch seeking (or able, if it so pleases him) to restrain the "extreme elements" among his "friends." The U.S. in relation to Israel in Lebanon (and the Middle East generally) or in relation to the death squads in El Salvador (along with whatever government is in power there) are examples of this. This is a tactic the U.S. imperialists have found useful and necessary in a number of situations, especially as a result of their defeat and exposure in Vietnam but also because of the imminence of world war, which means they can't get that deeply involved again — until it's time to go all the way.

The fact that they have the ability as well as the necessity to use this tactic has very much to do with the lopsidedness in the

[130] See, for example, Avakian, *For a Harvest of Dragons*, pp. 148-51; and Bob Avakian, "More on the Principal Contradiction in the World Today," *RW*, No. 172 (September 17, 1982), p. 8. On the controversy surrounding the nature and role of the Soviet Union see *The Soviet Union: Socialist or Social-Imperialist?*, Parts I and II (Chicago: RCP Publications, 1983).

world — the great difference (or gulf) between the oppressed countries and the imperialist countries that feast off and pillage them — and how this is reflected in the political realm: the much more ready and systematic use of terror, including open state terror, to "keep the people in line" and suppress resistance in the oppressed countries, while in the imperialist countries they can mask and "soften" the bourgeois dictatorship to a certain extent, particularly for more better-off sections of the people that are pacified to a significant degree with bribes from the imperialist spoils. The book *The Science of Revolution* sums this up in the following penetrating passage (speaking specifically of the U.S. bloc):

> The platform of democracy in the imperialist countries (worm-eaten as it is) rests on fascist terror in the oppressed nations: the real guarantors of bourgeois democracy in the U.S. are not the constitutional scholar and Supreme Court justice, but the Brazilian torturer, the South African cop, and the Israeli pilot; the *true* defenders of the democratic tradition are not on the portraits in the halls of the Western capitols, but are Marcos, Mobutu, and the dozens of generals from Turkey to Taiwan, from South Korea to South America, all put and maintained in power and backed up by the military force of the U.S. and its imperialist partners.[131]

Yet, on this very basis these imperialists seek to run a game, effecting a certain division of labor (or terror), to "skin the ox twice" politically (to use Lenin's phrase): achieving the brutal suppression in the colonies (or neocolonies) so necessary and essential to the functioning of their whole system — including for the bribing and pacifying of broad layers of the people in the "home country" — and at the same time acting as if they have nothing to do with all this terror, that they are surprised and horrified when it is brought to their attention, and if everyone will just leave everything to them they will try to see if they can influence those leaders "down there" (or "over there") to act more in accordance with American democracy, as soon as those trouble-

[131] Lenny Wolff, *The Science of Revolution: An Introduction* (Chicago: RCP Publications, 1983), p. 184.

some rebels, commies, and so on have been dealt with. To no small degree this game is played for the benefit of the more privileged strata in the imperialist countries — most of whom have never really felt the iron fist of bourgeois dictatorship — and those who are or aspire to be in a similar position within the oppressed countries themselves. Unfortunately, however, it also takes in more than a few people genuinely opposed to oppression, including some of the basic masses themselves.

All this stresses the need to thoroughly unmask the imperialists' decisive and determining role in these acts, to expose this sham and train people to see not just the hit man but the hand behind him, not just the "corrupt officials" but the Emperor. More, to see the connections and fundamental social and international relations involved and to wage a consistent, thoroughgoing struggle against this, on an international and internationalist level.

The Lesson of *Water Margin* and the Relation of Advance and Consolidation in the World Proletarian Revolution

As I argued in *For a Harvest of Dragons*:

> [T]he proletarian revolution (like everything else) proceeds not in an uninterrupted (if long-term) straight-line process, but through spirals; and just as it is absolutely essential to conquer as much as can be conquered in those periods when revolutionary possibilities are greatly accentuated, so it is absolutely essential to consolidate what has been won, especially when no more can be won for the time. Overall, advance is principal over consolidation, but advance and consolidation, being a unity of opposites, cannot exist without each other and are interrelated, so that there is no such thing as advance completely divorced from consolidation or advance which does not also demand consolidation, just as there is no consolidation without advance.[132]

[132] Avakian, *For a Harvest of Dragons*, p. 144.

Another aspect of this is that revolutions can only be made by making breakthroughs in particular countries (or areas) as the opportunities arise and by doing everything on the international level as well as within specific countries to be prepared for this — all guided by the overall orientation of making every possible contribution to the advance of world proletarian revolution as a whole. Or, as I put it in another context:

> [P]recisely in approaching things from the world scale, we have to be at one and the same time seeking to make the greatest advances in building the revolutionary movement and preparing for the development of a revolutionary situation in all countries, as a general principle — with the recognition that revolutionary situations can emerge and sharpen without much warning and seemingly unexpectedly . . . [and] be alert to particular situations which at any given point become concentration points of world contradictions and potential weak links, potential points where we can make a breakthrough, as the international proletariat, and where therefore the attention and the energy of the proletariat internationally should be especially concentrated at the given point.[133]

This, I believe, is the correct application of the basic point Stalin was speaking to when he said, "The front of capital will be pierced where the chain of imperialism is weakest, for the proletarian revolution is the result of the breaking of the chain of the world imperialist front at its weakest link."[134]

The proletarian revolution must be guided by internationalism and must be at bottom a *world* proletarian revolution to achieve the goal of a communist world, without which there can be no communism anywhere. But to think that this fundamental principle means that either the proletariat conquers the whole world *all at once* or it cannot (or even should not) conquer particular parts of it as that becomes possible is to deny the

[133] Bob Avakian, "Advancing the World Revolutionary Movement: Questions of Strategic Orientation," *Revolution*, No. 51 (Spring 1984), p. 26.

[134] J.V. Stalin, *The Foundations of Leninism* (Peking: Foreign Languages Press, 1970), pp. 29-30.

actual possibility of proletarian revolution at all. Or, as Lenin put it, "To wait until the working classes carry out a revolution on an international scale means that everyone will remain suspended in mid-air."[135] More, where breakthroughs are made, and once it must be summed up that no more can be won for the time being, internationally, then it is necessary to put the emphasis, for a time, on consolidating the gains that have been made.

On the other hand, a consistent fight has to be waged so that such a consolidation does not become strategic — that is, a thing unto and for itself, raised above instead of subordinated to the overall world revolution — which will mean that the gains made and consolidated will turn into their opposites: a reversal of the revolution and the loss of a base area for the world proletarian revolution. This is another important expression of the need to wage a consistent and all-around fight against the tendency to be against corrupt officials only and not against the Emperor — to strive only for a better place in the existing (and exploiting, oppressing) scheme of things, and in this case a better position in the imperialist division of the world — instead of carrying through with the protracted struggle to completely transform the whole world and uproot the basis for such a division, for imperialism itself, and for all such relations and conditions everywhere.

Some Lessons from the Roman Empire

A phenomenon associated with the decline and fall of the Roman Empire was that it was successively conquered by barbarians. But what is especially interesting and significant is that those barbarians who managed to install themselves as the ruling group generally became "Romanized" and "settled in."[136] On

[135] Lenin, "Report on Foreign Policy Delivered at a Joint Meeting of the All-Russia Central Executive Committee and the Moscow Soviet (May 14, 1918)," *LCW*, Vol. 27, p. 372.

[136] For more on this see Edward Gibbon, *The Decline and Fall of the Roman Empire*, in three volumes (New York: Modern Library, 1932).

the one hand this is an illustration of the principle Marx summarized, that "the mode of plunder is in turn itself determined by the mode of production,"[137] a case where a people with a less developed mode of production conquered another with a more developed one and basically adopted the latter as their own. But on the other hand there is an important lesson here for the proletariat and its struggle for a kind of society and world never seen before — one characterized by a high level of development of the productive forces (and their ongoing advancement to higher levels) but without class distinctions or the oppression of one part of society (or the world) by another.

The lesson here was actually suggested to me some time back in reading the remarkably insightful statement of an 11-year-old youth in Overtown (Miami) at the time of the rebellion there at the end of 1982:

> Well, the barbarians lived back in Roman times and the Romans were going all over the place ripping off people and the barbarians fought back. If they want to call us barbarians, okay, we'll be barbarians.[138]

"Tell 'em, put it back in their face!" was my immediate response in reading this (along with a smile of ironic satisfaction thinking of the many authorities and experts who had no doubt declared this kid "uneducable").

There is a great deal that revolutionaries can learn from the basic stand of this youth: the straight-up defiance, the willingness to take the worst that society can come up with to call you and embrace it as a badge of honor and a symbol that indeed you are, joyously, beyond the bounds — the bonds — of the established order and its laws. (Bob Dylan, many years ago now, wrote in one of his songs that "to live outside the law you must be honest," and in the same spirit I think we should add,

[137] Karl Marx, *Preface and Introduction to a Contribution to the Critique of Political Economy* (Peking: Foreign Languages Press, 1976), p. 28.

[138] Quoted in "On the Street in Overtown, From the Roman Empire to *What Is To Be Done?*," *RW*, No. 187 (January 7, 1983), p. 9.

especially in these times, that the reverse is certainly no less true: to be honest you must live outside the law.) At the same time, however, this set me to thinking that there is an important way in which we are different from the barbarians and that this too must be driven home to the advanced proletarians and the oppressed masses generally.

We are different *not* in that we don't want to tear down the system, defeating its armed forces on the battlefield to do so: without doing this it would be impossible to achieve any of our basic goals. No, this is our *similarity* with the barbarians. What is different — and it is a profound difference — is that the proletariat is not, and the leaders of the proletariat must not be allowed to become, new exploiters. Our historic mission is not to adopt — and adapt ourselves to — the old mode of production and its corresponding institutions and ideas but to make those two radical ruptures and bring into being something new and completely without precedent in human history: classless society, communism.

Continuing the Revolution Under the Dictatorship of the Proletariat, Carrying Through with the World Proletarian Revolution

Here my purpose is not to attempt to discuss this whole subject in depth or detail but to focus on three questions, summarizing some essential points.

(1) Mao's analysis, drawn from the positive and negative experience of the Soviet Union and China itself — that socialist society is a long transition period between capitalism and communism, all throughout which there are classes and class struggle; that the bourgeoisie is constantly regenerated out of the conditions (the contradictions) of socialism itself; that the more the socialist transformation advances the more the focus of this problem is within the vanguard party itself, especially at its highest levels where people in authority who take the capitalist road pose a great danger to socialism; and that this question

must be made known to the masses, indeed the means and methods must be developed to unleash their conscious activism in fighting against these capitalist-roaders and in continuing the revolution under the dictatorship of the proletariat at the same time as supporting revolutionary struggles worldwide — all this is a truly immortal contribution by Mao Tsetung to the theory and practice of proletarian revolution.

At the same time it is necessary to sum up that while this theory and political line of continuing the revolution under the dictatorship of the proletariat and above all the momentous struggle waged with the overall guidance of this line, the Great Proletarian Cultural Revolution in China, represent the highest pinnacle yet reached by the international proletariat, still "these things were treated a little bit as 'things unto themselves,' too much apart from the whole, worldwide struggle against imperialism, reaction, and all exploiting classes."[139] Even though support was extended to revolutionary struggles elsewhere and it was stressed that the final victory of a socialist country requires the victory of the world proletarian revolution, it was not firmly enough grasped and popularized that the socialist transformation of any particular country can only be a *subordinate* part of the overall world proletarian revolution.

(2) The question of "revolutionary successors." This is the question of bringing forward fresh forces for the revolution at every stage, especially *after* the seizure of power. There are two separate but interrelated aspects of this: developing mass forms for carrying forward the revolutionary struggle and raising the revolutionary consciousness of the masses on the one hand and on the other bringing forward and training new leaders of the proletarian revolution and finding the ways and means to keep them "red" — on the road of revolutionary communism. In both cases, this requires fighting the "calcification" and conservatism that tend strongly to set in once some initial gains have been

[139] Bob Avakian, "On the Philosophical Basis of Proletarian Internationalism," *RW*, No. 96 (March 13, 1981), p. 3.

made in transforming society — and, frankly, in improving the situation of the majority of the people — gains which will become a powerful basis for a reversal of the revolution if they are made into things unto themselves and the goal becomes above all to preserve and protect them — and extend them — without the willingness to risk losing them. This, too, in the final analysis is "Ah Q-ism," not revolutionary communism.

(3) All this has a great deal to do with the question of really, fully practicing proletarian internationalism: keeping the world revolutionary movement as the highest priority, challenging people on that basis and level, keeping constantly mindful of the fact that even where power has been seized in a particular country that is only the first step of many thousands that must be taken in the world proletarian revolution and making this a mass question, a question to be thrashed out broadly — and deeply — throughout society. This is especially important in a country like the U.S., most of whose people have for decades enjoyed, to one degree or another, "perks" from living in a powerful imperialist country, a world predator with the resultant high level of productive forces and standard of living. Not only in this present and crucial period but even more so after U.S. imperialism has been brought down and a revolutionary regime established on its ashes, the orientation of linking revolution from the beginning and consistently with the revolutionary struggle and revolutionary transformations in other parts of world, especially (what is now) the Third World, must be fought for — and this fight carried through.

In a fundamental sense, let the young barbarians *remain* barbarians and not become new Romans. Let them be real rebels, outlawed in the reactionary world order until there is no longer any such order to outlaw them; let them not become Sung Chiangs fighting to get and then accepting the offer of "amnesty and enlistment" with the Emperor.

* * * * *

I would like to end the second part of this book on a personal note — which, however, is not merely personal but has much larger political implications: Billy, I'm still not drinking Coke (in the largest sense).

Here I'm referring to an old friend of mine, Billy Carr, whom I knew from high school and kept contact with until he was shot dead ten years ago, a victim of the system even though he died in a dispute with petty criminals over who cares what. Growing up in the ghetto in Berkeley (yes, there is a ghetto in Berkeley!), he was forced into a situation of bouncing back and forth between the bottom layers of the proletariat and the criminal life of the lumpen proletariat, yet he never lost a largeness of mind and a searching for some other way, some other kind of world. Whenever I could I sought him out to talk with — both to learn and to discuss with him the things I was learning as I got involved in political movements, began to see more clearly the nature of the beast we are up against and got turned on to revolution. Many years ago, in discussing South Africa and the role of the U.S. in relation to it, I pointed specifically to the major role of Coca-Cola in South Africa and told him I had decided not to drink Coke as a personal protest. After that, every time we talked one of the first things he would ask is: "Are you still not drinking Coke?" Though I eventually gave up this particular form of protest as ineffective, and he understood that, his question still had a much larger meaning, and we both knew that. And, in that spirit, this has remained a question I continue to ask myself, to make sure I can continue to say: No, I'm still not drinking Coke — in the largest sense.

In its larger implications, this is another illustration of the importance of a vanguard party, which is especially crucial in this period — of the fact that, through the whole upsurge of the '60s not just in the U.S. but internationally, and persevering and becoming tempered and steeled through the '70s and into the '80s, there is a leadership actually capable of being the guiding center in preparing for and carrying out the overthrow of U.S. imperialism. There is a party that is not only the vanguard of the revolutionary proletariat in the U.S. but is a part of an international force fighting for the world proletarian revolution, the Revolutionary Internationalist Movement.

III.

The Dictatorship of the Proletariat, the Goal of Communism, and the Role of Dissent

The Relation Between the Dictatorship of the Proletariat and Truth — And Between Changing and Knowing the World

There *is* such a thing as objective truth, though it can never be completely known — objective reality can never be fully reflected in human thought — because the universe is infinite and infinitely changing. On the other hand, as I pointed out in a pamphlet on the role and importance of the vanguard party and of party-building: "The philosophical underpinning of bourgeois democracy is agnosticism and eclecticism, 'There's no truth anyway, so the important thing is that the majority of people have their will.' But the problem is that there is truth. That is, even truth as understood correctly as a contradictory phenomenon, a thing advancing through motion and development, or through contradiction."[140]

Knowledge is accumulated in spirals, involving the continuous interaction and interpenetration between practice and theory — in which the former is principal overall — but also involving leaps from one level to another. Knowledge is acquired, humanity does add to its store of knowledge, but not in a continuous, unbroken straight line. As argued in *Mao Tsetung's Immortal Contributions*, the state or store of acquired knowledge — what can be determined to be true — at any stage must be taken as the foundation from which to struggle to acquire further knowledge (even though that further knowledge involves

[140] Avakian, *If There Is to Be Revolution, There Must Be a Revolutionary Party*, p. 17.

discarding or correcting part of the previous "state or store of acquired knowledge"). Without this one plunges into relativism, a form of idealism (nothing is objectively true, it is all ideas...one opinion is as good as another...and so on), and the very process of acquiring knowledge, of knowing and changing the world, is fundamentally disrupted.

Mao Tsetung makes clear:

> Marxists recognize that in the absolute and general process of development of the universe, the development of each particular process is relative, and that hence, in the endless flow of absolute truth, man's knowledge of a particular process at any given stage of development is only relative truth. The sum total of innumerable relative truths constitutes absolute truth.[141]

But at the same time Mao notes:

> As man's practice which changes objective reality in accordance with given ideas, theories, plans or programmes, advances further and further, his knowledge of objective reality likewise becomes deeper and deeper. The movement of change in the world of objective reality is never-ending and so is man's cognition of truth through practice.[142]

Yet, again, this process, like everything in life, proceeds in a spiral, and "to say at any point, 'Well, tomorrow we will know more than today, so let's not (dogmatically) apply what is known as truth today,' is to deny and disrupt the process by which more knowledge is actually acquired."[143]

It is impossible to arrive at an all-around understanding of the truth (at any given point) without the correct outlook and methodology. Marxism-Leninism-Mao Tsetung Thought is that outlook and methodology. In *For a Harvest of Dragons* I pointed

[141] Mao, *On Practice*, *MSW*, Vol. 1, p. 307; see also Avakian, *Mao Tsetung's Immortal Contributions*, pp. 154-58.

[142] Mao, *On Practice*, *MSW*, Vol. 1, p. 307.

[143] Avakian, *Mao Tsetung's Immortal Contributions*, p. 156.

out: "What is most controversial, however, is Marxism's claim to be not just a science but an all-encompassing science, a single, unified worldview and methodology that provides a comprehensive approach to analyzing — and synthesizing — and to changing reality, both nature and society."[144] But as I also pointed out in that work, Marxism is nevertheless just such a worldview and methodology. At the same time I emphasized that it is in fundamental contradiction to Marxism to claim that it has solved every problem, once and for all, and has brought about complete and final knowledge of reality. For as Mao puts it, Marxism "has in no way exhausted truth but ceaselessly opens up roads to the knowledge of truth in the course of practice."[145]

It is also impossible to arrive at the truth without centralism — leadership (though this will take a qualitatively different form in communist society). All ideas should not get "equal time" nor *could* they, under any social system or set of circumstances. There has to be some means for determining what will be given priority, what will be posited as true, and what will be focused on as a target of criticism. What these means are and whether they correctly reflect material reality as fully as possible will depend on the social system. Further, it is impossible not only to arrive at an all-around understanding of the truth but to make it a material reality without social struggle — which means above all class struggle in class society.[146]

The interests and outlook of the proletariat and the proletariat alone — as a class and not speaking merely of particular leaders or parties as such — are fully in accord with grasping and wielding the truth to change the material world (including society and people) in accordance with its basic laws. In this, the

[144] Avakian, *For a Harvest of Dragons*, p. 42.

[145] Mao, *On Practice*, *MSW*, Vol. 1, pp. 307-8, cited in Avakian, *For a Harvest of Dragons*, p. 43.

[146] These are points I focused on in "Some Questions to Carl Sagan and Stephen Jay Gould," *RW*, No. 180 (November 12, 1982), p. 3 and "More Questions to Carl Sagan, Stephen Gould, and Isaac Asimov," *RW*, No. 207, p. 3, in the series *Reflections and Sketches* and *More Reflections and Sketches*, respectively.

interests and outlook of the proletariat are in fundamental contradiction and locked in acute conflict with the dominant, reactionary relations, institutions, and ideas. In *For a Harvest of Dragons* this basic principle is summarized this way:

> [T]he outlook of the proletariat, the scientific worldview and methodology of Marxism, unlike all other class outlooks, is not only partisan, it is also true. It represents a class outlook but it is not blinded or prejudiced by class *bias*. This is because of the fact that the position and role of the proletariat in society and human history are radically different from those of any other class. The proletariat carries out socialized production in a society (and world) marked by large-scale industry, the widespread application of science, highly developed means of communication, etc.; it is the exploited class in capitalist society, a society split in the main into two directly antagonistic classes, the bourgeoisie and the proletariat; because of its propertyless condition it is subjected to domination and exploitation by capital and subordinated to the dynamics of capitalist accumulation, and its interests lie in the thorough revolutionization of society, in bringing about the most radical rupture with traditional property relations and traditional ideas, as it is put in the *Communist Manifesto* — the proletariat can emancipate itself only by abolishing not just capitalism but all exploitation, indeed all class distinctions and their material and ideological bases. It is for this reason that Marxism openly proclaims its class character and ruthlessly exposes the class character and interests in all relations, institutions and ways of thinking in present-day (and past) society.[147]

It is not that truth itself has a class character.[148] Nor still

[147] Avakian, *For a Harvest of Dragons*, p. 44.

[148] When we wrote, in our polemics over the revisionist coup in China: "In other words truth has a class character and there are certain universal truths of Marxism-Leninism," we were in error with regard to the first half of that statement. What we were getting at is that different classes have fundamentally different approaches to the question of truth and only the outlook and methodology of the proletariat is capable of correctly reflecting reality in a comprehensive, thoroughgoing way. Still, this statement that "truth has a class character" is wrong and reflects some confusion on this important point. See Revolutionary Communist Party, *Revolution and Counterrevolution* (Chicago: RCP Publications, 1978), p. 267.

less should truth be directly equated (and sometimes it should not be equated at all) with the governing ideas and policies of any particular proletarian state at any given time (even a *genuine* socialist state) to say nothing of a nonproletarian, reactionary state, whether openly such or in "Marxist" disguise.

But to fundamentally know and change the world (including society) in accordance with its basic laws, Marxism-Leninism-Mao Tsetung Thought must be in command as the guiding orientation and methodology, and politically the proletariat — in a concentrated way through its vanguard party but through its own mass initiatives and struggles as well — must lead in the struggle to grasp and apply the truth in the process of changing the world. Otherwise reactionary class forces and ideology will occupy the commanding posts, obscure the truth, keep knowledge — flawed, corrupted, and crippled knowledge (at best) — the province of an elite and impose reactionary economic and social relations throughout society.

The first great step — or leap — in enabling humanity, through its social organization, to know and change the world consciously on the basis of a correct comprehensive worldview and method is the seizure of political power by the proletariat and the establishment of the dictatorship of the proletariat to suppress the overthrown bourgeoisie and other counterrevolutionary elements and to unleash the suppressed energy, initiative, and creative potential of the masses to transform society. But this is after all only the first step: the revolution must be continued, broadened, and deepened. In socialist society, the class struggle continues, including as a very important dimension the class struggle in the ideological realm. And this class struggle, conditioned itself by the overall world situation and international struggle, exerts a tremendous influence on and in the final analysis determines whether or not objective truth will be grasped and made a powerful material reality, and whether or not a whole new society — and world — will be achieved where class divisions do not fetter society and people and distort and vitiate the struggle to know and use the truth, in accordance with the basic laws of the universe. The truth does not automatically "win out" nor automatically "set you free": those who represent the truth must battle and defeat those who obscure the truth and obstruct its application; and so long as society is divided into classes, this means class struggle — ideological, political, and ultimately military.

The development of the class struggle greatly influences not only the accumulation of knowledge but also the relationship between centralism and democracy (diversity. . .dissent) in socialist society. This too is a question of spiral-like development. This question — the relation between centralism and democracy, between a leading line and diversity of thinking, between authority and dissent — does not pose itself the same way at all times, nor can it be handled with exactly the same policies in all situations. There is a question of necessity and freedom — their dialectical interrelation — involved here (which, again, is fundamentally determined by the overall world situation and struggle and also, as a key part of this, by the class struggle in the socialist country itself).

It is in this light that we can fully appreciate the significance of Mao's statement, seven years after nationwide political power had been won in China:

> In a great revolution embracing 600 million people, the masses would not have been able to rise if we had not killed off such local despots as the "Tyrant of the East" and the "Tyrant of the West." *Had it not been for that campaign of suppression, the people would not have approved our present policy of leniency.*[149]

And the same basic principles are involved in Lenin's insistence, during the touch-and-go days of the civil war after the October 1917 insurrection in Russia:

> The chief accusation made against us by the European petty bourgeoisie concerns our terrorism, our crude suppression of the intelligentsia and the petty bourgeoisie. "You

[149] Mao, "On the Ten Major Relationships," *MSW*, Vol. 5, p. 298, emphasis added.

> and your governments have forced all that upon us," we say in reply. . . .
>
> . . . And we shall be the first to take steps to confine it to the lowest possible minimum as soon as we put an end to the chief source of terrorism — the invasion of world imperialism, the war plots and military pressure of world imperialism on our country.[150]

However much it may be incomprehensible to many in the intelligentsia and many bourgeois democrats generally, however much this kind of approach may madden them, Mao and Lenin are correct, profoundly so.[151]

Leninism is Better than Bourgeois Democracy

Lenin's contributions to and in fact his qualitative development of Marxism have made him the focus of attack from many quarters, an attack that continues down to today, and not only from the imperialists and other open counterrevolutionaries but also from many who claim to be opposed to the capitalist system. Lenin's theory and practice concerning the need for a disciplined vanguard party and the relationship between this party and the broad ranks of the proletariat (and other masses)

[150] Lenin, "Eighth All-Russia Conference of the R.C.P.(B.)," *LCW*, Vol. 30, pp. 180-81.

[151] Of course it could be argued that, even after the immediate emergencies had passed and power was firmly consolidated, this question of giving more freedom to the intellectuals, allowing more diversity, etc., was never correctly handled in the Soviet Union or China. While fundamentally disagreeing with this, I do believe there are certain respects in which some errors have been made in the experience of the proletarian dictatorship in this regard, and in any case it remains one of the more difficult problems to handle correctly and requires deeper summation — this basic question will be returned to shortly.

It might also be objected that in saying that there is necessity and freedom involved in this question of centralism versus democracy, diversity, dissent, etc., I am saying nothing different from what is said by all ruling regimes and their spokesmen — that they will allow dissent so long as it doesn't really threaten them. But there is a world — and a worldview — of difference between the basic approach and methodology, as well as the basic objectives, of the proletariat and the bourgeoisie (and other reactionary classes) on this question — a point which will also be returned to shortly.

has been at the heart of the conflict, and *What Is To Be Done?*, the work where Lenin most systematically addresses these questions, is a special target of criticism. As I pointed out in *For a Harvest of Dragons*:

> It is not without reason that opportunists. . .along with openly reactionary political commentators, analysts, scholars, "dissidents" from the Soviet empire, and even some honest but confused people who have taken radical political stands but have not yet overstepped the bounds of bourgeois democracy, all single out *What Is To Be Done?* for attack. In particular they focus on its insistence on distinguishing between the masses, and their spontaneous consciousness, on the one hand, and class-conscious revolutionaries on the other — and more specifically on the conclusion that there must be an organized vanguard of the proletariat, with a backbone of professional revolutionaries, that brings communist consciousness to the masses from outside the sphere of their immediate economic relations and their economic struggles. This orientation, it is said, is the source of the degeneration of the revolution in Russia, of the establishment of a "dictatorship of the party over the masses," and so on.[152]

In that book I gave a more lengthy response to this attack, as well as others, on *What Is To Be Done?* and the whole thrust of Lenin's line, especially concerning the role of the party and its relation to the masses. Here I believe that the following two sentences can stand as a concentration of that response:

> Lenin's argument in *What Is To Be Done?* — that the more highly organized and centralized the party was, the more it was a real vanguard organization of revolutionaries, the greater would be the role and initiative of the masses in revolutionary struggle — was powerfully demonstrated in the Russian Revolution itself and has been in all proletarian revolutions. Nowhere has such a revolution been made without such a party, and nowhere has the lack of such a party contributed to unleashing the initiative of the masses of oppressed in *conscious revolutionary struggle*.[153]

[152] Avakian, *For a Harvest of Dragons*, p. 74.

[153] Avakian, *For a Harvest of Dragons*, p. 84.

I would be very much interested to see a serious attempt to refute this argument — especially what is said in the last sentence above — or to declare that it is beside the point!

To sharpen up the point here, it is helpful to look more specifically at the kind of attacks on Lenin that are voiced by people who fall into the general category of "honest but confused people who have taken radical political stands but have not yet overstepped the bounds of bourgeois democracy." In the U.S., Noam Chomsky is, I believe, a good example of this, and examining the attempts to portray Lenin as a dictatorial elitist in Chomsky's book *Towards a New Cold War*, in particular the first chapter, "Intellectuals and the State," will shed considerable light on the problem.[154]

Let us only note in passing the howling contradiction and almost hilarious irony that Chomsky cites Bakunin as a pathbreaker in warning of the dangers not just of a new intellectual-technocratic elite in industrial society but specifically of a "red bureaucracy." Bakunin was a nineteenth-century anarchist and opponent of Marx and surely the holder of a legitimate claim to be one of the most manipulative and "elitist" men in the history of revolutionary movements.[155] Chomsky's main point here is to identify what he calls "a new class of scientific intelligentsia," and the fact that in regards to its influence and inclinations there is a "kind of convergence, in this regard at least, between so-called socialist and capitalist societies."[156] The blame for this, of course — at least from the side of the "so-called socialist societies" — lies with Lenin and his insistence on subordination to centralized authority. So argues Chomsky.

[154] Noam Chomsky, *Towards a New Cold War* (New York: Pantheon Books, 1982), Chapter 1: "Intellectuals and the State," pp. 60-85.

[155] One is forced to ask if Chomsky has ever read such works as Bakunin's *Catechism of a Revolutionist*, a bible indeed for manipulation and machination by "revolutionary elites." I confess to having read it, many years ago now, when I was being turned on to revolution by the Black Panther Party; Eldridge Cleaver, who always retained a strong streak of the lumpen hustler and "jack-up artist" in him, was enthusiastically promoting this "Catechism."

[156] Chomsky, *Towards a New Cold War*, p. 63.

To buttress this argument, Chomsky first cites a statement by Lenin in 1918 — or more accurately, *part* of a statement by Lenin — and then a statement in 1920 in the following way:

> "*unquestioning submission* to a single will is absolutely necessary for the success of labour processes that are based on large-scale machine-industry. . . today the Revolution demands, in the interests of socialism, that the masses *unquestioningly obey the single will* of the leaders of the labour process" (emphasis in original); "there is not the least contradiction between soviet (i.e., socialist) democracy and the use of dictatorial power by a few persons." And two years later: "The transition to practical work is connected with individual authority. This is the system which more than any other assures the best utilization of human resources."[157]

Chomsky immediately follows this with a quote from Robert McNamara — a "typical example of the scientific and educational estate in state capitalist democracy" — except Chomsky does not inform us that it is McNamara who is being quoted until after we read the latter's statement, apparently to highlight Chomsky's assertion that leaving aside a reference to God in the statement by McNamara, "it would be hard to tell" whether the quote is from McNamara or Lenin.[158]

Even if one were to agree that there is the striking similarity in these statements by Lenin and McNamara that Chomsky claims to see (and I do not think there is, even with a rather superficial reading), what Chomsky is doing here must be called

[157] Chomsky, *Towards a New Cold War*, p. 63.

[158] Chomsky, *Towards a New Cold War*, p. 64. The statement by McNamara, as Chomsky quotes it, is as follows: "Vital decision-making, particularly in policy matters, must remain at the top. God — the Communist commentators to the contrary — is clearly democratic. He distributes brain power universally, but He quite justifiably expects us to do something efficient and constructive with that priceless gift. That is what management is all about. Its medium is human capacity, and its most fundamental task is to deal with change. It is the gate through which social, political, economic, technological change, indeed change in every dimension, is rationally spread through society. . . the real threat to democracy comes not from overmanagement, but from undermanagement. To undermanage reality is not to keep it free. It is simply to let some force other than reason shape reality. . . if it is not reason that rules man, then man falls short of his potential."

out for what it is: cheap demagoguery. The following are some of the main things wrong with Chomsky's method and conclusions:

(a) He doesn't indicate the *historical context* for these statements by Lenin. In 1918 the Soviet Republic was in its infancy and locked in a literal war for its survival with imperialists and counterrevolutionaries seeking to strangle it in the cradle. (Lenin's 1920 statement cited by Chomsky will be addressed shortly.)

(b) The quotes — in particular the first one — are cut up and separated from the overall "flow" of Lenin's discussion. Chomsky does not quote Lenin's remarks, *from the same paragraph* in the 1918 article, that:

> Given ideal class consciousness and discipline on the part of those participating in the common work, this subordination would be something like the mild leadership of a conductor of an orchestra. It may assume the sharp forms of a dictatorship if ideal discipline and class consciousness are lacking.[159]

Nor does he quote Lenin's statement, *also in the same paragraph*,[160] with regard to the achievement of a situation where people do unquestioningly obey the single will of the leaders of labor:

> Of course, such a transition cannot be made at one step. Clearly, it can be achieved only as a result of tremendous jolts, shocks, reversions to old ways, the enormous exertion of effort on the part of the proletarian vanguard, which is leading the people to the new ways.[161]

[159] Lenin, "The Immediate Tasks of the Soviet Government," *LCW*, Vol. 27, p. 269.

[160] Perhaps the reason Chomsky presents these quotes in such a mutilated manner is that he has not read the original statements by Lenin. In pursuing this I discovered that Chomsky's footnote for this contains only the reference "Cited by Maurice Brinton, *The Bolsheviks and Workers' Control* (London: Solidarity, 1970)" (see *Towards a New Cold War*, p. 399). But if Chomsky did fail to consult the original source while basing his case on these statements by Lenin, as he took them from another source, that is hardly better than if he did consult the original and still presented the quotes in this cut-up form.

[161] Lenin, "The Immediate Tasks of the Soviet Government," *LCW*, Vol. 27, p. 269.

(c) Chomsky acts as if this is the first and last thing Lenin had to say about such questions, as if Lenin insisted on the subordination of the masses to bureaucrats, technocrats, and party hacks, and that's all there is to it. The truth is that during the period from the victory of the October Revolution to his death, only seven years later, Lenin paid a great deal of attention to and agonized over the problem of how to combat bureaucracy in the state apparatus, how to increasingly involve the masses in the administration of the state and in political affairs generally, and how to fight against those forces that were seeking to bring about the restoration of capitalism, in league with world imperialism. Anyone seriously looking into this question could not help but come across numerous speeches, articles, and other writings of Lenin dealing with these questions and their concrete manifestations at different points. For example, in "A Great Beginning" in 1919 (i.e., the year in between the dates of the statements Chomsky cites) Lenin praised and popularized the subbotniks — involving volunteer labor by workers consciously working for the benefit of society and not their individual gain — and in so doing stressed:

> The communist organization of social labor, the first step towards which is socialism, rests, and will do so more and more as time goes on, on the free and conscious discipline of the working people themselves who have thrown off the yoke both of the landowners and capitalists....
>
> The nonproletarian and semiproletarian mass of the working population cannot but recognize the moral and political authority of the proletariat, who are not only overthrowing the exploiters and suppressing their resistance, but are building a new and higher social bond, a social discipline, the discipline of class-conscious and united working people, who know no yoke and no authority except the authority of their own unity, of their own, more class-conscious, bold, solid, revolutionary and steadfast vanguard.[162]

[162] Lenin, "A Great Beginning," *LCW*, Vol. 29, pp. 420, 423.

And, later that year, Lenin summed up:

> The lesson is that only workers' participation in the general administration of the state has enabled us to hold out amidst such incredible difficulties, and that only by following this path shall we achieve complete victory. . . .
>
> If you recall the past, if you recall the first steps of Soviet power, if you recall the entire work of developing all branches of the administration of the Republic, not excluding the military branch, you will see that the establishment of working-class rule two years ago, in October, was only the beginning. Actually, at that time, the machinery of state power was not yet in our hands, and if you glance back over the two years that have since elapsed you will agree with me that in each sphere — military, political and economic — we have had to win every position inch by inch, in order to establish real machinery of state power, sweeping aside those who before us had been at the head of the industrial workers and working people in general.[163]

Again, some people, apparently Chomsky included, may not understand that there is a unity between the masses of workers mastering and transforming the state apparatus on the one hand and the vanguard leadership ousting and replacing opportunists in positions of leadership on the other hand. Yet that unity is not only real but essential all the same.

While the point could be illustrated with innumerable references to the works — practical as well as theoretical — of Lenin, I will cite just one more here, Lenin's summation in 1920 of "one of the most profound and at the same time most simple and comprehensible precepts of Marxism":

> The greater the scope and extent of historical events, the greater is the number of people participating in them, and, contrariwise, the more profound the change we wish to bring about, the more must we rouse an interest and an intelligent attitude towards it, and convince more millions and tens of millions of people that it is necessary. In the final

[163] Lenin, "Two Years of Soviet Rule," *LCW*, Vol. 30, p. 129.

> analysis, the reason our revolution has left all other revolutions far behind is that, through the Soviet form of government, it has aroused tens of millions of people, formerly uninterested in state development, to take an active part in the work of building up the state.[164]

Are these, as well as others like them, statements that, except for, say, references to "the Soviet form of government," someone like Robert McNamara would or could make?

(d) It is true that Lenin did advocate one-man management ("individual authority") in industry and argued that this was not in contradiction to socialist democracy, as in the 1920 statement quoted by Chomsky. But here too Chomsky acts, first of all, as if this can be divorced from Lenin's overall view of the masses' decisive role in ruling and transforming society under socialism, as indicated by the statements I have cited, and further as if Lenin's ideas on economic management and the relation of managers to the mass of workers in production were the "last word" of Leninists on this question. Surely, Chomsky must know that no less a Leninist than Mao Tsetung summed up, from the experience of the Soviet Union and China itself, that one-man management was in fact a vestige of capitalism and a hindrance to the socialist transformation of the economy and society as a whole; that under Mao's leadership mass forms of management (revolutionary committees) were developed together with concrete policies to involve managers and other intellectual workers in productive manual labor and other steps to begin breaking down the division of labor left over from the old society. And why, when he is purporting to identify Leninism with capitalism on the role of intellectuals and other "elite" strata and their relation to the masses, does Chomsky not deal with the Great Proletarian Cultural Revolution in China, the greatest mass upheaval and conscious mass activism yet witnessed, which focused to a large degree on struggle over these very questions and broke entirely new ground in these spheres?

[164] Lenin, "The Eighth All-Russia Congress of Soviets," *LCW*, Vol. 31, p. 498.

All in all, Chomsky's handling of this question is stunningly irresponsible. And this is, frankly, rather shocking given that Chomsky is someone who places great emphasis on intellectual integrity — and in particular the lack of it among the intellectual elites of contemporary society, in both the Soviet and the U.S. blocs — someone who is a genuine, merciless, and in many ways penetrating critic of the present order and its ideological prostitutes and hatchet men. In fact, the very kind of irresponsibility (and even "cheap shot-ism") that Chomsky displays in his attempts to misrepresent Leninism as the ideology of a "red bureaucracy" is one of the targets Chomsky most subjects to withering exposure and repudiation in his work overall. How to explain this glaring contradiction?

An insight into this is given in the comment of a bourgeois historian on one of the background sources he drew from: "when his own religion is not involved, [he] shows a discriminating judgment."[165] Chomsky's "religion" is bourgeois democracy — of a particular, fairly radical anarchist-tending type — a major tenet of which is opposition to Leninism. And it is this — that is, bourgeois-democratic class bias and prejudice — that has caused him to lapse into such misbegotten methods in seeking to discredit Leninism. This is yet another demonstration of the fact that it is only of Marxism-Leninism-Mao Tsetung Thought that it can be truthfully said: "It represents a class outlook but it is not blinded or prejudiced by class *bias*." It is a vivid illustration of the principle that while the truth itself has no class character and is not a class question in that sense, *arriving* at it, in an all-around way, most definitely is!

Marx's Profound Insight

In *The Eighteenth Brumaire of Louis Bonaparte*, Marx wrote, "The bourgeoisie, to be sure, is bound to fear the stupidity of the

[165] William H. Prescott, *History of the Conquest of Mexico and History of the Conquest of Peru* (New York: Modern Library), p. 19.

masses as long as they remain conservative, and the insight of the masses as soon as they become revolutionary."[166] This not only incisively describes the attitudes of the bourgeoisie (though the reference to fearing the stupidity of masses that are *conservative* applies more to a bourgeoisie that is still more or less a rising class historically and retains some elements of opposition to reaction, as did the bourgeoisie in France and other parts of Europe in the period Marx was writing about); it also brilliantly describes the attitudes of bourgeois-trained intellectuals, particularly the more progressive-thinking ones. And this applies to their attitudes toward the class-conscious revolutionary proletariat not only before it gets to the point of seizing power but also — and in certain ways even more so — after it has seized power and is running society.[167]

One of the sharpest expressions of this is the common attitude among the intellectuals that the proletarians are too crude and unsophisticated to lead in intellectual fields in particular — the arts and sciences, etc.[168] However, the proletariat must lead

[166] Karl Marx, *The Eighteenth Brumaire of Louis Bonaparte*, *Karl Marx and Frederick Engels Selected Works* (Moscow: Progress Publishers, 1973) p. 480.

[167] Mao, in discussing this question, eight years after nationwide political power had been won in China, noted that among the nonparty intellectuals, "some have read a few Marxist books and think themselves quite learned, but what they have read has not sunk in, has not taken root in their minds, so that they don't know how to use it and their class feelings remain unchanged. Others are conceited; having picked up some book-phrases, they think themselves terrific and are very cocky; but whenever a storm blows up, they take a stand very different from that of the workers and the great majority of the working peasants. They waver while the latter stand firm, they equivocate while the latter are forthright" (Mao, "Speech at the Chinese Communist Party's National Conference on Propaganda Work [March 12, 1957]," *MSW*, Vol. 5, p. 425).

[168] As Mao put it in 1958: "Last year the rightists brought up this question and created a lot of trouble. They claimed that the nonprofessional could not lead the professional"; but, Mao said, "The nonprofessional leading the professional is a general rule" (Mao, "Speeches at the Second Session of the Eighth Party Congress [May 8-23, 1958], *Miscellany*, Part I, p. 110). Otherwise different "professions" become compartmentalized, along with the knowledge acquired in them — since most people are "professional" only in their "own field" — and there is no way to fully synthesize and apply the general principles underlying and running through different fields of activity and knowledge. Anyway, most bourgeois-trained intellectuals do take leadership (however reluctantly or grudgingly in some cases) from nonprofessionals already — bourgeois political authorities!

in these fields anyway, although to do so the proletariat and its politicians must learn to be both firm and flexible, piercing to the heart of problems while having a sense of the complexities involved, criticizing their own errors and boldly correcting their mistakes, including the tendency to handle things too crudely and roughly — mechanically.

Most intellectuals are of course not hopeless. Besides their negative side many of them also have a positive one and a positive role to play, though this depends on overall conditions. Many are attracted to the proletarian movement and to the critical, revolutionary stand of the class-conscious proletariat — especially, to be frank, when there is a serious crisis in society *and* when the revolutionary movement of the proletariat is powerful. The strategic orientation toward them, both before and after the proletariat has seized power, must be to unite and to struggle with them so as to enable them to make important contributions to the socialist transformation of society and the international struggle leading to a communist world and to the advancement of humanity. This will be a long-term and complex problem, also proceeding in a spiral-like motion, but in order to carry out its historic mission the revolutionary proletariat must learn how to master this too.

Overcoming the Division of Labor of Class Society and Knowledge as Capital

The historic task is to overcome the division of labor characteristic of class society — overcome it in the fullest and most all-around sense, with the masses really becoming masters of society in every practical sphere and every sphere of knowledge, taking all this into their own hands and under their own direction. Any other way, precisely what you will have is the installation of an intellectual elite and the dictatorship of those who monopolize the spheres traditionally blocked off to and inaccessible to the masses.

At every stage throughout this process — throughout the

entire transition to communism when, finally, the material basis for this will no longer exist — there will be people who oppose the struggle and motion toward overcoming this division of labor, and people who specifically try to turn knowledge into capital — all of which will be a powerful force favoring capitalist restoration in socialist society itself. As Mao argued in criticizing a Soviet political economy textbook (even before he had fully developed his analysis of classes and class struggle under socialism):

> Page 461, paragraph 2, says, "In a socialist national economy science's latest achievements, technical inventions, and advanced experience can be popularized in all enterprises without the slightest difficulty." This is far from necessarily so. In a socialist society there are still "academic overlords" who control the organs of scientific research and repress new forces. This is why science's latest achievements are not simply popularized without the slightest difficulty. Such a manner of speaking essentially fails to recognize that there are contradictions within a socialist society. Whenever something new appears it is bound to meet with obstacles, perhaps because people are unaccustomed to it or do not understand it, or because it conflicts with the interests of a particular group.[169]

It is also true that the force of habit and tradition, interacting with the remaining aspects of the old division of labor, weighs on the masses and has an intimidating effect, hindering them from taking up and conquering the "forbidden" areas of intellectual knowledge, technical expertise, and so on. This is another aspect of why the masses cannot fully become masters of society without leadership, without a vanguard party: a contradiction, a very sharp contradiction, but one which can only be handled by finding the ways to revolutionize the party as part of the overall process of revolutionizing society and carrying forward the world proletarian revolution above all — and not by

[169] Mao, *A Critique of Soviet Economics*, p. 74.

denying the need for leadership and abandoning or undermining the vanguard role of the party.

If the goal of overcoming the old division of labor and abolishing the basis for class divisions in society is to be achieved, it will be as a result of determined class struggle. Under socialism this struggle will become very acute and will even immediately determine the direction of society — forward toward a communist world or backward to capitalism — at certain "concentration points" (again, linked most fundamentally to the overall world situation and struggle). It will require encouraging and enabling the masses themselves to thrash these things through and struggle them out together with but also at the head of the intellectuals — even at the cost of certain short-term "losses" (in particular in developing specialized or technical expertise, in making technological advances, etc.) and even if at times the masses mishandle things or "make a mess of things." Or else, again, it will be impossible to overcome these divisions between mental and manual laborers and the overall division of labor characteristic of class society, and these "mental" spheres will remain the monopoly of an intellectual elite, serving an exploiting class — in whatever guise, even "socialism" or "communism."

That the transition to communism, the struggle against capitalist restoration and in particular the fight against the consolidation of an intellectual elite monopolizing crucial spheres of knowledge, requires the leadership of a vanguard party may be ironic — and, as noted, it is definitely a profound contradiction — but it is not the willful invention of power-seeking, bureaucracy-installing Leninists. It is rather the case that the very division of labor that must be struggled against and finally overcome gives rise, so long as it has not yet been overcome, to the need for a vanguard, and "the contradiction between the vanguard and the masses becomes a concentrated expression of the contradictions that make the vanguard necessary in the first place."[170] The only way forward in the face of this is to find the

[170] Avakian, *If There Is to Be Revolution, There Must Be a Revolutionary Party*, p. 2.

ways to wage revolutionary struggle — increasingly conscious mass revolutionary struggle — to move toward the goal of abolishing this division of labor and the very basis for class distinctions, whereupon not only the need but the possibility of a vanguard party distinct from the masses will disappear. And if the goal ceases to be to overcome these distinctions — not only in a particular country, even a socialist country, but above all in the world as a whole — and becomes instead to preserve, reinforce and extend these divisions, then an exploitative class society can only result.

Throughout the socialist transition the leading role of a vanguard party and its unleashing and guiding of the initiative and conscious activism of the masses — while learning from and being tempered and in a fundamental sense "supervised" by this — corresponds to the necessary forms and relations of democracy *and centralism*, just as the need for the dictatorship of the proletariat is an expression of the still existing class contradictions and antagonisms and their underlying material basis in socialist society, which can only be a transition to communism and is not yet classless society itself.

It is useful and vital even now to project ahead and grapple with the problem of how these questions will be handled in communist society. This is essential in order to maintain and develop the largeness of mind and sweeping historical view and the "critical edge" that must characterize communists and also to sharpen our revolutionary insight into and grasp of the current stage of the struggle and its relation to the future goal.[171]

In the late 1930s Mao Tsetung wrote in *On Practice*, "The epoch of world communism will be reached when all mankind voluntarily and consciously changes itself and the world."[172] But, especially with the further experience in socialist society and the contradictions and struggles there, Mao also stressed repeatedly

[171] In this regard, it is worth mentioning again the novel *The Dispossessed*, by Ursula LeGuin, which makes a serious effort to grapple with some of these questions and provides many provocative insights.

[172] Mao, *On Practice*, *MSW*, Vol. 1, p. 308.

that communist society too would be marked by contradiction and struggle, though not antagonistic class struggle. For example: "Will there be no struggle when we get to communism? I just don't believe it. There will be struggles even then, but only between the new and the old, between what is correct and what is incorrect. Tens of thousands of years from now, what is wrong still won't get by, it won't stand up."[173]

Clearly, then, "all mankind voluntarily and consciously changing itself and the world" in communist society, while it will and must be carried out without class dictatorship or state coercion, will not be possible without the kind of struggle, often sharp struggle, that Mao alludes to. How will this contradiction be handled? Obviously it would be impossible at this stage of history to do more than sketch the broadest outlines of this, but one thing that will definitely be true in communist society is that there will remain the relationship and contradiction between collectivity and diversity, between agreed upon actions and directions on the one hand and individual (or group) initiative on the other, between what is held to be true and ongoing struggle to deepen — or correct, or even discard — this, and so on. And in this sense, there will still be the need for some kind of leadership, or centralized guidance, and there will be the contradictions involved in effecting this without giving rise to new elites, to the seeds of class polarization and state coercion. Both economically and politically such "centralism" will be necessary, unavoidable, but it will be no less necessary and unavoidable to see to it that such centralism does not become the institutionalized role of particular individuals or groups (rotating people through different responsible positions is one measure that will have to be applied, but others will have to be developed as well) and that "leadership" or particular areas of knowledge and activity do not become the "preserves" (or "strongholds") of particular people or groups who show a specific inclination toward

[173] Quoted in Yao Wen-yuan, *On the Social Basis of the Lin Piao Anti-Party Clique*, (Peking: Foreign Languages Press, 1975); also in *Peking Review*, No. 10 (March 7, 1975), reprinted in Lotta, ed., *And Mao Makes* 5, p. 204.

pursuing that field.

In any case, communism will not be — society never has been, never could be, and never will be — characterized by "pure democracy" (in fact democracy is a category of class society and as such will disappear when classes are eliminated). Nor will communist society recognize the uninhibited right of individuals to do whatever they want: in fact individuals will, in the overall sense, still be subordinate to society as a whole — though *not* to other individuals. How this will be handled without resorting to coercion or the suppression of individual initiative will surely be a process of trial and error and a focus of sharp struggle.

But in all this it should be kept in mind that these questions, while they can and should be taken up and wrangled over even now, are bound to be viewed to a significant extent, even by communists, through the prism of present-day society and its relations, values, and ideas. In fact, however, the stage of communism, where such questions can be finally taken up as immediate, practical problems for solution, will only be achieved through truly monumental and world-historic struggle, changing circumstances and people in radical and unprecedented ways, so that in the future communist society the conditions and people of today, when studied, will seem as unlikely and almost incomprehensible as the thought is now of a world where such things are completely alien.

The United Front Strategy as a Long-Term Orientation, and the "100 Flowers" and "100 Schools" as a Long-Term Policy

Lenin pointed out in *"Left-Wing" Communism, An Infantile Disorder*:

> The abolition of classes means not only driving out the landlords and capitalists — that we accomplished with comparative ease — it also means *abolishing the small commodity producers*, and they *cannot be driven out*, or crushed; we *must live in harmony* with them; they can (and must) be

> remolded and reeducated only by very prolonged, slow, cautious organizational work.[174]

This principle must also guide the strategic orientation and approach to the intellectuals, who generally speaking hold the same class position in society as the small producers and have the same class outlook, fundamentally, though they play different roles and may differ, even sharply in some respects, in terms of their specific inclinations, habits, ways of looking at things, and prejudices. Here it is helpful to recall the statement by Marx that one must not imagine

> that the democratic representatives are indeed all shopkeepers or enthusiastic champions of shopkeepers. According to their education and their individual position they may be as far apart as heaven from earth. What makes them representatives of the petty bourgeoisie is the fact that in their minds they do not get beyond the limits which the latter do not get beyond in life, that they are consequently driven, theoretically, to the same problems and solutions to which material interest and social position drive the latter practically. This is, in general, the relationship between the *political* and *literary representatives* of a class and the class they represent.[175]

For these reasons, the united front must remain the strategic orientation for both "living in harmony with" but also remolding and reeducating the petty bourgeoisie, including the intelligentsia, through the socialist transition period; and for these reasons too, this must be a united front *under firm proletarian leadership.*

With regard to the arts and sciences (and the intellectuals involved in them), which have their own particularities, a basic orientation must be that formulated by Mao Tsetung as "Let a Hundred Flowers Blossom, Let a Hundred Schools of Thought

[174] Lenin, *"Left-Wing" Communism, An Infantile Disorder* (Peking: Foreign Languages Press, 1965), p. 32.

[175] Marx, *The Eighteenth Brumaire of Louis Bonaparte*, p. 424.

Contend."[176] And, as Mao also advocated, this must be a long-term policy, because, as he explained,

> it often happens that new, rising forces are held back and sound ideas stifled. Besides, even in the absence of their deliberate suppression, the growth of new things may be hindered simply through lack of discernment. It is therefore necessary to be careful about questions of right and wrong in the arts and sciences, to encourage free discussion and avoid hasty conclusions.[177]

(It is also important to note Mao's comment in the same speech that "many of our comrades are not good at uniting with intellectuals. They are stiff in their attitude towards them, lack respect for their work and interfere in certain scientific and cultural matters where interference is unwarranted.")[178]

This is a very difficult problem to handle correctly, because, among other things, in socialist society too people with specialized knowledge or ability in these fields will try to turn that into capital and preserve such areas as the domain of a privileged few, shutting the masses out and refusing the overall guidance and leadership of the party, *even when* that leadership is not crude or stiff. In 1950, Stalin wrote: "It is generally recognized that no science can develop and flourish without a battle of opinions, without freedom of criticism."[179] But in practice Stalin did not do so well in applying this. This is linked to some larger methodological problems on Stalin's part, including a tendency to treat Marxism-Leninism as a static, absolute truth, combined with a certain pragmatism: truth = what is needed at the moment, in narrow terms (for example, the "Lysenko Affair," where Stalin intervened to support erroneous scientific theories and suppress opposition to them, in large part because

[176] See, for example, Mao, "On the Correct Handling of Contradictions Among the People," *MSW*, Vol. 5, p. 408.

[177] Mao, "On the Correct Handling of Contradictions," *MSW*, Vol. 5, pp. 408-9.

[178] Mao, "On the Correct Handling of Contradictions," *MSW*, Vol. 5, p. 404.

[179] J.V. Stalin, *Marxism and Problems of Linguistics* (Peking: Foreign Languages Press, 1972), p. 29.

of the exigencies of agricultural production). But Stalin's problems in this arena were also due in no small measure to the fact that he was dealing with what is an extremely complex and difficult problem: how to give "air" to the intellectuals and encourage creativity, critical thinking, initiative, and the "battle of opinions" while at the same time leading the intellectuals — when they by and large do *not* readily accept such leadership or embrace the Marxist outlook and method.

How to handle the dialectical relationship between "100 flowers" and "100 schools" on the one hand and on the other hand the need for the proletariat to (in Mao's phrase) "exercise all-round dictatorship over the bourgeoisie in the realm of the superstructure, including the various spheres of culture"?[180] This is similar to the phenomenon that while truth itself does not have a class character, the struggle to grasp and apply it is most definitely a class question — a question of class struggle — in class society. All-around dictatorship does not mean crude imposition of whatever the current policies of the government are. It does mean that the Marxist method must be in command and leadership must be in the hands of those who have demonstrated the ability to grasp and apply it — in a *critical* way, without turning it into a static, sterile state religion. This too will be a question of sharp struggle. Take, for example, how we will deal with something like graffiti art and artists under socialism. Certainly we will not seek to suppress them and to wipe away their works; but *neither* should we try to "pacify" and "sanitize" them by simply giving them assigned places to do their work, etc. — though there will be a place for that. But beyond that, we should enter into this arena with them, seeking to learn and to criticize, right on the same walls and other places where they are creating — if their shit's no good, artistically and/or politically, then let's tell them and everybody so and make it a mass question if they don't dig our criticism; and especially if it *is* good, ar-

[180] Mao, "Chairman Mao on Continuing the Revolution Under the Dictatorship of the Proletariat," *Peking Review*, September 26, 1969; quoted in Avakian, *Mao Tsetung's Immortal Contributions*, p. 199.

tistically and politically, let's let everybody know that too and support and popularize it, without "legitimizing the life out of it"! Variety, diversity in art is very important; without this, creativity would be stifled, and on the other hand creativity will bring forth variety and diversity — though the artists' self-expression is not more important than the content and social effect of their art (which are principal and decisive through all the different forms in which art is expressed).

Either the Marxist method and proletarian forces — concentrated through the party but also involving the masses and mass initiative broadly — will be in command and leading in the arts and sciences (and the superstructure generally) or the opposite methodology and forces will: classes do and will sharply contend over this, so long as classes (and their social basis) exist. One class or another must win out. There is no "pure" knowledge or search for knowledge (and no "art for art's sake" standing outside or above class contradiction and struggle), just as there is no "pure" democracy (without class content). But fortunately, *one* of these methodologies does provide a comprehensive basis for arriving at, and making a powerful material force of, the truth: the outlook and interests of the proletariat do correspond to the further emancipation and enlightenment of humanity, in a qualitatively greater way than ever before.

This touches on the question of "thinking for yourself." While it has some value to the degree that it implies criticial rather than slavish thinking, this notion is ultimately a truism (everyone thinks and can only think with his/her own brain and not anyone else's) and/or it is a fundamental falsehood: everyone's thoughts are based largely on indirect knowledge, facts and concepts presented (in "distilled form") by *others*. This is especially obvious in a society where the media and means of communication generally play such an influential role. The essential question is not "thinking for yourself" but thinking according to *what method* — a correct or incorrect one — leading to what *basic result* — truth or falsehood.

"Marxism Is a Wrangling *Ism*"

Why must the revolutionary proletariat favor, encourage, and foster the "battle of ideas," the critical spirit, and the challenging of convention — dissent in that basic sense — in socialist society no less than in capitalist society? This is not a question of some kind of concession to the intellectuals but fundamentally a means for furthering the struggle of the masses themselves to master and transform society in every sphere in accordance with the interests of the proletariat and the advance to communism — and it is a question of how communism itself is conceived. Criticism and the battle between the new and the old and between right and wrong are essential to Marxism itself. As Mao said, "Marxism is a wrangling *ism*, dealing as it does with contradictions and struggles."[181]

Ideas need challenging. Even wrong ideas or incorrect criticism may raise important questions, besides the fact that criticism of prevailing ideas may be correct. The masses — as well as party members and especially the leaders of the party and the state under socialism — need to be exposed to controversy and the struggle over conflicting ideas and criticism of and challenges to accepted ideas and norms. This is certainly no less necessary under socialism than in capitalist society. And when we are in power we must struggle to maintain the same willingness — no, more, eagerness — we have now to take on and demolish through exposure and debate counterrevolutionary or just plain wrong ideas, theories, and so on.

In several previous works I have cited Mao's summation that in the Soviet Union in the 1920s, when they didn't have anything to rely on but the masses, they had a much more lively spirit, including in how Stalin gave leadership, but later on after they accumulated some gains they basically got ideologically lazy. I think this is one of the most important problems that has

[181] Mao, "Talks at a Conference of Secretaries," *MSW*, Vol. 5, p. 364.

to be understood and that struggle has to be waged around — the tendency, even sometimes when you're not literally in control of a society but when you've achieved a certain position relative to others, to become lazy ideologically, to rest on your laurels and to react to criticism or challenges with, "Who the hell are these upstarts and what the hell have they ever done and where are their credentials?" or "Everybody knows these people are counterrevolutionaries so we don't have to bother refuting them," and so on. This, again, is one of the most harmful attitudes that can take hold in a movement, in a party, and especially of course in a party that is in the position of leading a socialist state.

As for our party and other revolutionary communists today, we're like those leaders in the Soviet Union in the '20s — we don't have anything to rely on except our taking these ideas out and thrashing them out, our critical daring and our taking the decisive questions to the masses. And that's why, or at least this has a great deal to do with why, we have such an eagerness — "Bring us a fucking reactionary idea, we're ready." Today we seek out every opportunity for this but it will be a little different when we've accumulated some gains. Then there will be the tendency to sit on these gains and become conservative and rely on what's been accumulated and not on the challenges and the obstacles yet to be tackled and overcome. This is going to be a very sharp struggle: we're not helpless in the face of this, but the problem has to be identified and the basis has to be laid even now to wage that struggle in the future, especially where political power is won.[182]

[182] Why should we revolutionary communists be afraid of the reactionaries? I have fantasies about a movie I'd like to make (not that I think it would be a great work of art — but it would be fun and have some value — let it be a little work of art). I'd like to take all these things like this movie *Sudden Impact*, where they have Clint Eastwood as Dirty Harry, revived again: "Go ahead — make my day!" My idea is that we would make such people reenact these roles — those that are still around after the proletariat has seized power. So we have Clint Eastwood up there, "Make my day." OK — boom! We'd change the scene so in the film he gets righteously blown away. And the movie would go on with about thirty or forty of the most infuriating scenes like that, but changing the endings to give real satisfaction. Such scenes as they are now are not only

All this is related to the crucial question of overcoming the division of labor left over from capitalism and previous class-divided societies. The radical rupture with all that could hardly be accomplished without tradition-challenging, convention-breaking initiative and without ferment and upheaval in socialist society, certainly involving the criticism of, shaking up, and in some cases the pulling down of leading people.

But the point is to arrive at the truth and change the world to advance society and emancipate humanity — not for everyone to have their say as some abstract principle. And such wrangling, criticizing, challenging, and so on — such diversity and dissent in that sense — is *not* the same as *pluralism.* Pluralism is a bourgeois concept, a rationalization or camouflage covering the actual imposition by the ruling class and its representatives of a definite class outlook and methodology — an erroneous, reactionary outlook and methodology — on every question of any importance, every serious struggle over ideas. In fact, pluralism

---

infuriating because they're reactionary, they're doubly infuriating because they're so ridiculous. Clint Eastwood (Dirty Harry) would have been blown away ten times in this bank scene before he even got to his pocket. Such scenes are infuriating artistically as well as fundamentally politically. So my idea would be to force them to reenact such scenes and put the appropriate ending on them. But with humor.

This goes along with another idea, or fantasy, I've had: to bring out all these hacks, warhorses, and ideological prostitutes in the media, etc., and make them read their news reports (their contention for the "with a straight face award") — their endless barrage of reactionary propaganda — force them to read this stuff in front of meetings of revolutionary masses, masses who have become politically conscious and hip to all this. The purpose would be to subject these hacks to perhaps the most stunning and difficult punishment of all for them — the anger and ridicule of the masses. Especially the ridicule. Ridicule is a powerful weapon.

I just can't understand why revolutionary communists should be defensive in the face of such people! If you listen to them, they have absolutely nothing (that is, no real arguments) to stand on and they only rely on the fact that they have state power and a lot of guns and weapons of mass destruction behind them. That's what the ultimate substance of their argument always is: "If you don't like it, then how about this argument" (the tanks, aircraft, missiles, and nuclear arsenals that are the "bottom line" of their arguments). We should not rely on such things as *our* ammunition in ideological struggle when we have state power. I say, bring 'em on, one and all — though with some organization, priorities, etc. They want to whine about how they're going to be suppressed and not even allowed to speak up — well, let 'em speak up. But we're going to determine the context in which they speak up and in that context we're going to *make* them speak up, and let's have some fun while we thoroughly dissect and destroy their outmoded, rotten and vicious theories, credos, nostrums, and bromides.

can very well serve the interests of a ruling class that exercises its dictatorship in a bourgeois-democratic form: it can even allow a few things to slip through in the media, works of art, etc., that oppose the status quo while surrounding, overwhelming, and smothering them with the dominant ideas, theories, and values.

Pluralism as such is an expression of agnosticism, which — wrongly — denies objective truth. That is, it denies such truth on one level while actually defining truth (openly or implicitly, consciously or "by default") as whatever is in accord with and serves the outlook and interests of the ruling class. (This is closely akin to the pragmatism that is upheld and promoted by the U.S. imperialists especially.)

In fact, such pluralism is the same in essence as state Marxism = state religion, the ruling ideology in the revisionist countries (with the social-imperialist Soviet Union the outstanding example). The difference is only in form: the revisionist "Marxists" proclaim their religious dogma as absolute, exhausted truth, unchanging — or changing frequently but only and always in accord with the momentary interests and requirements of the revisionist ruling class and always a rigid "law" for as long as that is useful — always ponderous but brittle. Truth, in short, according to these revisionists and their apologists, is whatever it is said to be at any given time by those in power (and "defining phenomena" to suit their narrow and particular interests as an exploiting class in "socialist" and "communist" guise). Orthodoxy is always their watchword. "Orthodoxy can be as stubborn in science as in religion," as Stephen Jay Gould has noted.[183] And this *certainly* applies to revisionist pseudoscience. On the other hand, the "pluralists" say (at best) that the conflict of opinions and ideas itself is more important, higher than objective truth — or even that there *is no* objective truth, only different points of

[183] Stephen Jay Gould, *The Panda's Thumb* (New York: W.W. Norton & Company, 1982), p. 243.

view, with each as true (and untrue) as the other.[184] But in the final analysis the "pluralists," by acting as if all ideas are equal and can compete equally — when in reality the bourgeois ruling class has a monopoly on the dissemination of ideas and exercises dictatorship in the realm of ideas, as it does in every other sphere — actually aid this ruling class in defining and enforcing as truth whatever suits its own class interests and outlook.

The communist viewpoint and methodology is of course fundamentally opposed to both of these wrong and class- (bourgeois-) biased outlooks and methodologies (which, again, are the same in essence though differing in form). With a communist understanding the point of the conflict over ideas (the "wrangling" Mao referred to) is to arrive at a correct synthesis *and* be able to *act* on this to further change the world. (This relates back to the discussion on the relation of the dictatorship of the proletariat and truth.) The reason and purpose of communists in encouraging and unleashing this wrangling over ideas, the critical spirit, the challenging of convention, the dissent from the established norms, is that this is in accordance with the basic laws of development of all life and society and with the interests of the proletariat, which must also *lead* all this to contribute in various ways to the advance to communism. This is possible only with the establishment of Marxism in the commanding position and the exercise of the all-around dictatorship of the proletariat — in the way summarized here, and in particular in dialectical unity with the long-term policy of "100 flowers" and "100 schools."

[184] A revealing example of this is the bourgeois-democratic legal process with its court procedures; taking them at their best, they are founded on agnosticism and relativism — the most important thing is not arriving at the truth but the "due process" itself, and in fact this very process in itself works against arriving at the truth.

IV.

The Future of Humanity:

Certain Questions of Historical Importance and Urgent Application for the International Communist Movement and Others Seeking to Radically Change the World

More Thoughts on the Basic Orientation Toward Proletarian Revolution

It might seem that we revolutionary communists are "back where we started," even hurled back to where we were after the defeat of the Paris Commune over 100 years ago, since today there are no socialist states and, worse, those that existed have experienced a restoration of capitalism. But this is a superficial view, refuted by materialist dialectics.

In terms of the objective factor — the objective world conditions — the contradictions of the world imperialist system and the struggles these give rise to, driven forward by the underlying fundamental contradiction of capitalism (between socialized production and private appropriation) and its laws of accumulation, have continued to propel things toward the resolution of these contradictions and the final elimination of capitalism (and all exploiting systems and relations). As a result, even though proletarian revolutions have been defeated or reversed, the material foundation for proletarian revolution has been strengthened and from a world-historic standpoint things have been brought closer to the achievement of communism, despite all the distortions and lopsidedness in world economic and political relations.[185] This of course is not to say that the motion toward world communism (alone among things in the universe) will proceed in a straight line, nor is it to deny the possibility of dramatic leaps *backward* at a given point. But with all that, the basic point that objectively the basis for communism is being

[185] Here it is worth recalling the comment from our party's Central Committee Report, five years ago, that even if imperialism hangs on for several hundred years more, the world will then be that much riper for communist revolution and the predictions of Marx and Engels will be vindicated (see "The Prospects for Revolution and the Urgent Tasks in the Decade Ahead, Documents from the Third Plenary Session of the Second Central Committee of the RCP,USA," *Revolution*, Vol. 4, Nos. 10-11 [October/November 1979], p. 15).

strengthened, despite setbacks and reversals in the world proletarian revolution, remains true.

Of course it requires revolutionary struggle led by the proletariat to actually make the leap to socialism in different parts of the world and then to communism on the global level. And such revolutions greatly accentuate world contradictions and accelerate the motion toward the replacement of the epoch of capitalism with the epoch of world communism.

In terms of the subjective factor — that is, the conscious, organized forces of proletarian revolution — there is a great deal of accumulated experience, positive and negative, to learn from. There is a rich revolutionary legacy, which must be upheld at the same time as it is critically evaluated and critically assimilated. This corresponds to reality: the experience of proletarian revolutions so far should be mainly upheld and secondarily criticized, though criticized and dissected fearlessly, penetratingly, and thoroughly. And we have the scientific principles and methods to guide us — to enable us to synthesize the lessons more thoroughly and apply them systematically in the decisive period ahead — the science of Marxism-Leninism-Mao Tsetung Thought, which is itself the theoretical reflection of the rich experience of the past 100 years and more of the world revolutionary movement as well as a basic comprehensive outlook and methodology. But we must not simply defend Marxism-Leninism-Mao Tsetung Thought. We must apply it and further develop it, because it is, once again, a living science in which there is a unity and a constant interplay between upholding its basic principles and further enriching them through critically approaching, evaluating, and synthesizing new experiences and developments and the lessons which must be drawn from them.

Finally, as discussed before, the "revolutions gone sour" — in particular the defeat and reversal in the Soviet Union and then in China — are bitter losses, but they are only *part* of the overall development of this spiral toward its explosive concentration point (conjuncture). They are not the end of the spiral — or the "end of the story."

The fact is we are not back to "nothing" and everything

should not be called into question. Nor again is this the time for "quiet reflection" or "slow patient work"! The formation and the *Declaration* of the Revolutionary Internationalist Movement represent a great victory, a great weapon for the international proletariat and the international communist movement in approaching this conjuncture and a powerful refutation of such erroneous views.

Again on the Importance of Grasping the Spiral/Conjuncture Motion of Imperialism

Not only do things in general develop in spirals, but there is a particular motion to the working out of world contradictions in the stage of imperialism, in which at certain historical points these contradictions are especially tightly interwoven and heightened, leading to a dramatic explosion and then resolution (though partial and temporary) involving a qualitative recasting of world relations — among the imperialists, and between them and the forces opposed to them. At least this is how spiral motion under imperialism has gone on up to this point and is going on now, approaching another — and by far the most dramatic — world-historic conjuncture. In this process, world wars have so far been the nodal points. Stalin's observation concerning World War 1 has great relevance for today's world situation: "The significance of the imperialist war which broke out ten years ago lies, among other things, in the fact that it gathered all these contradictions into a single knot and threw them on to the scales, thereby accelerating and facilitating the revolutionary battles of the proletariat."[186]

In today's world situation there is an immediate and urgent application of and importance to this. We are heading into just such a world-historic conjuncture and one where the resolution

[186] Stalin, *The Foundations of Leninism*, p. 6. A thorough analysis of this most crucial question of the spiral/conjuncture motion under imperialism is outside the scope of this book. Such an analysis has been made in *America in Decline*, Vol. 1, in particular the first chapter: "Political Economy in the Epoch of Imperialism and Proletarian Revolution," pp. 21-169.

of this will involve a more earthshaking change, one way or the other, than has ever been witnessed.

It is crucial, then, to grasp this spiral/conjuncture motion in its sweeping historical dimension and as a basic orientation — including the fact that in a fundamental and overall sense the development of the world proletarian revolution has so far taken place as part of this motion and its "rhythm," although revolutionary struggles and especially successful proletarian revolutions have reacted back on the underlying motion of capitalism in this stage of imperialism, sometimes decisively so. Without this understanding it will be impossible to grasp the acuteness and urgency of the present world situation and to act to decisively affect it and qualitatively change its present direction — through revolution.

One major question that is highlighted in this connection is the importance of a thorough rupture with the nationalist tendencies in the history of the international communist movement — the tendency to view the world through the prism of one's particular country and to see the revolutionary struggles in the rest of the world as essentially external and secondary to what is happening in the homeland. (An exception of sorts to this has been the tendency to transfer the same sort of allegiance to a socialist fatherland which is not one's own country. But in this case the same sort of nationalism is applied to that socialist fatherland — it is seen as standing above and more important than the world revolutionary movement as a whole.)

Without a thorough rupture with such nationalist tendencies it is not possible to have a truly, fully global approach, which is necessary not only to strengthen the communist movement at the international level and the unity between revolutionary struggles in different countries but also to recognize and concentrate on making breakthroughs at "weak links" in the world imperialist system as they develop, sometimes suddenly and seemingly without warning. This does not run counter to but is in dialectical unity with the fact that, as the *Declaration of the Revolutionary Internationalist Movement* says, the communists in different countries have the particular "responsibility of leading the revolution in each country in the sense of each party's share in the preparations and acceleration of the world revolution."[187]

All this is very much related to the problem that, as I put it in *Conquer the World*, "there is a limit . . . to how far you can go in transforming the base and superstructure within . . . [a given] socialist country without making further advances in winning and transforming more of the world."[188] (Once again it should be said that a thorough analysis of this question is beyond the scope of this presentation; besides what is discussed in *Conquer the World*, important aspects of the theoretical basis for this analysis are found in *America In Decline*, in particular in chapter one. Here I will try to summarize the essential points.)

It is true that there is such a limit — although this limit is not absolute and unchanging and cannot be "fixed" in the abstract — precisely because the imperialist system has highly integrated the world economy (though not uniformly and evenly) and socialist countries cannot help but be significantly involved in and influenced by this. More fundamentally, it is because in this era the basic underlying contradiction determining the development of world relations and the changes in them — which in turn are decisive in determining the development of the class struggle and the emergence or intensification (or mitigation) of revolutionary situations in particular countries — is the contradiction fundamental to capitalism, between socialized production and private appropriation, with its two essential expressions: the contradiction between anarchy and organization in production and the contradiction between the bourgeoisie and the proletariat (and their respective allies). In other words, in an imperialist-dominated world changes within particular countries have become integrated into a single overall world process, in which the fundamental contradiction of capitalism is the underlying force determining the development of things. And within this, the contradiction of anarchy versus organization in

[187] *Declaration of the Revolutionary Internationalist Movement*, p. 46.

[188] Avakian, *Conquer the World*, p. 38.

production — understood in the broadest sense and on an international scale — is overall the driving force, generally setting the framework for the class struggle, although the class struggle and especially revolutions do significantly react back upon the process as a whole and its underlying basis, and at times can become the driving force.

As much as they represent a qualitative change in the economic relations and the political/ideological superstructure within the particular country and in the relations between it and the rest of the world, socialist revolutions and the ongoing transformations in socialist society cannot escape the overall world framework. They are significantly, indeed in the final analysis decisively, conditioned in their development by the overall world situation and the struggles and changes within it — which include of course revolutionary struggles and successful revolutions that actually seize parts of the world from imperialism. Thus, for all these reasons there is a limit to how far the advance can be carried within a particular socialist country without winning and transforming more of the world. This is an important aspect of the material basis not only for proletarian internationalism in general but for why the defense of a socialist country and the carrying forward of revolutionary transformations there, while of tremendous importance, must be subordinated, overall, to the world revolutionary movement as a whole. Therefore, *necessary* risks have to be taken with regard to a particular socialist country and its defense if and when there is a realistic prospect of making further advances for the international proletariat, including decisive breakthroughs at a given point.

The working out of the present spiral, the approach of this particular world-historic conjuncture, and the stakes involved — including the very real question of nuclear devastation and annihilation of most of civilization as we know it — and the tasks this puts before us, while they do *not* change the basic nature of the process and the contradictions propelling it, or the means of resolving it in the interests of the masses worldwide (and ultimately of humanity itself), do nonetheless have some profoundly new and different features than in the past. This demands specific, urgent attention and emphasis — that is, emphasis on preventing world war — which must include particular tactical measures that flow from and serve this objective. But most fundamentally we must continue to prepare for and accelerate the one thing that can prevent such a war (along with striking at the source of all the other outrages and evils in society): revolution, led by the proletariat and aimed at the overthrow of imperialism and reaction.

Some Questions to Ponder

With today's world situation, including the special and urgent aspects referred to, and with the difficult period and difficult struggle the international communist movement has been passing through (especially with the loss in China, following not that long after the triumph of the revisionists in the Soviet Union and capitalist restoration there), might we say that we revolutionary communists are passing through our "Long March" on the international level: a crucial turning point with the opportunity and the pressing necessity to find the ways to turn serious defeat into world-historic advances in the face of the gravest danger yet posed? And might we consider the formation of the Revolutionary Internationalist Movement a crucial turning point within this (as was the uniting of the leadership of the Chinese Communist Party around the correct line shortly before the conclusion of the Long March)?

Some Thoughts About the Special Problems of Revolution in Revisionist Countries

"Going Back to Yenan"

On several occasions, in the context of discussing the danger of imperialist attack on socialist China and/or the seizure of power by revisionists within China itself, Mao raised the prospect of "going back to Yenan" (which was the headquarters of the Chinese Communist Party and its armed forces from the mid-1930s through the war against Japan and until the time in the late 1940s when Chiang Kai-shek's forces were swept from mainland China and the People's Republic of China established). For example, in a speech at a Central Committee meeting in 1958 Mao said that if there should be a war against China and major cities like Peking and Shanghai were occupied, "we will resort to guerrilla warfare. We will regress one or two decades and return to the Yenan era."[189]

While Mao's basic stand and orientation here are important, and inspiring, a serious question arises in this connection: Is it really possible to "go back to Yenan" in the broadest political (and economic) sense? And if you did "regress one or two decades and return to the Yenan era," how easy would it then be to return again to the present era? Would the peasant masses once again support you, after they have already been through the stage of getting land in the land reform and then the stage of basic land collectivization? What about the more privileged urban middle classes and even many workers who have tended to become more conservative as their lot has greatly improved under socialism? And if these different strata were rallied in support, on what basis would that be?

The common denominator and probably the major motivating factor for most would be patriotism if it were a case of foreign invasion, but that is not the same thing as support for socialism. Experience has shown — in particular in the case of the Soviet Union — that it is possible in a socialist country to fight and win a patriotic war and yet *weaken* the basis of socialism (a point I addressed in *Conquer the World*).[190] And if it is a case not of a foreign invasion but of revisionists "at home"

[189] Mao, "Speech at the Sixth Plenum of the Eighth Central Committee (December 19, 1958)," *Miscellany*, Part I, p. 147; see also Mao, "Example of Dialectics (Abstracted Compilation)," *Miscellany*, Part I, p. 222.

[190] Avakian, *Conquer the World*, especially pp. 22-28.

seizing power and promising more material benefits and personal gain — "after all isn't that what the revolution was fought for in the first place?" they will say — how easy will it be to lead masses back to the mountains to wage a difficult war to overthrow these revisionists? All this poses a vexing problem that must be pondered and studied more deeply, and wrangled over.

The "Generation Problem" in Socialist Countries

Mao noted in the early 1960s that a problem in socialist countries is that the children of party and state functionaries tend to have a relatively privileged position and therefore to be conservative.[191] (He also commented, "In the Soviet Union, it was the third generation that produced the Soviet Khrushchev Revisionism.")[192] This, it seems to me, is a general problem that is bound to develop — and not only among the children of cadres but even among sections of the masses — because socialism does (and should) bring an improvement in the lives of the people. But it is a problem that is accentuated to the degree that the essential nature, purpose, and aims of the revolution are presented in terms of improving the position of the country in the world and improving the livelihood of the people in the country — to the degree, in other words, that nationalist and economist tendencies exert influence. In socialist society it is above all the children of those bourgeois democrats that have become capitalist-roaders who are inclined to become grasping philistines steeped in bourgeois cynicism.

The Soviet Bloc

The negation of revisionism, even when that assumes the form

[191] See Mao, *A Critique of Soviet Economics*, p. 117 and Mao, "Reading Notes," *Miscellany*, Part II, pp. 306-7.

[192] Mao, "Cultivating Successors to the Revolution," *Miscellany*, Part II, p. 357.

of mass rebellion, is not — immediately — the reclaiming of Marxism. A major reason for this is that the status quo, the established order, and institutionalized power being rebelled against, wear the mantle of Marxism. Poland is a concentrated example of this (students rebelling for the right to have crucifixes in the schools — what a perversely twisted world we live in, right now especially!). The problem is how to transform a rebellious but bourgeois-democratic negation of revisionism into a revolutionary negation of capitalism and the bourgeoisie in *all* their forms, disguised and open. This raises certain tactical questions especially connected with the development of a proletarian revolutionary movement in the revisionist countries, in Eastern Europe in particular.

As pointed out in the *Declaration of the Revolutionary Internationalist Movement*, while the emergence of a socialist camp after World War 2 was a powerful reality and overall a significant advance in the struggle against imperialism — and this was particularly because of the role and influence of socialist China after 1949 — this socialist camp

> was never solid. Little revolutionary transformation was carried out in most of the Eastern European Peoples' Democracies. In the Soviet Union itself powerful revisionist forces unleashed going into, in the course of, and in the aftermath of the Second World War grew in strength and influence.[193]

With the triumph of revisionism in the Soviet Union in the mid-'50s, following the death of Stalin, those Eastern European countries where little revolutionary transformation had been carried out became part of the Soviet imperialist bloc in which they occupy a subordinate position even though some of them are advanced capitalist countries themselves (more industrially developed than the Soviet Union in certain cases) and are on the imperialist side of the basic division in the world between im-

[193] *Declaration of the Revolutionary Internationalist Movement*, p. 21.

perialist countries and oppressed countries. Because of these particularities,

> in the countries of Eastern Europe Marxist-Leninists face the task of formulating correct strategy and tactics for the socialist revolution, taking into account the domination of Soviet social-imperialism and the concrete tasks it poses without minimising or overlooking the central task of overthrowing the state power of their own bureaucratic bourgeoisie.[194]

The situation and the tasks with regard to these Eastern European revisionist countries is a peculiar and sharp example of the principle that Marxism will have to be brought to the masses "from without" (in this case this largely means from literally outside their borders and is a kind of extension into another arena of the basic truth that Marxism must be brought to the masses from outside their own immediate experience). The "spilling over" into Eastern Europe of resistance and protest in the West (in particular the antiwar and antinuke movements) is an important illustration of the need both to transform these protests and rebellions into a powerful revolutionary movement — including a revolutionary defeatist stand toward the Western bloc and "one's own" imperialism — and to work consciously to spread *this* influence "to the East." It is already crucial that leaps be made in this sphere — in the political and ideological interpenetration between West and East *and* the strengthening of the revolutionary communist current within this. This could be a decisive part of the revolutionary struggles and revolutionary victories that could prevent world war, which means actually overthrowing some imperialist states and shattering and reordering European relations on *that* basis and as part of the overall world proletarian revolutionary movement. And even in order to make significant "inroads" and have a powerful impact politically and ideologically on the Eastern European countries,

[194] *Declaration of the Revolutionary Internationalist Movement*, p. 43.

spurring the development of the struggle against the imperialists of both blocs and their war preparations, a revolutionary thrust from the West is necessary.

Taking Responsibility for the Future of Humanity

Changing the international political map and striving to prevent world war through revolution: actually seizing power through mass revolutionary struggle in as many places as possible — even making a revolutionary breakthrough to seize power in one country or another — is the crucial step that will reverberate throughout the globe like an earthquake under the whole structure of world relations. This is the key link in setting off a whole "chain reaction" in these world relations — which will not only batter and shake the entire edifice of world imperialism at its foundations but as a particular aspcct of this will also be a powerful force stimulating revolutionary struggle toward the overthrow of the ruling bourgeoisie in the revisionist countries (in particular of the Soviet social-imperialist bloc but including China and others as well), undermining their whole "logic," their raison d'être and the basis of their "practical" appeal to many revolutionary or potentially revolutionary forces.

All this is a very important application of the statement by Marx that while theory is crucial and revolutionary ideas taken up by the masses can become a tremendous material force, still material force must be defeated by material force and the weapon of criticism can never equal the criticism of weapons.

If, on the other hand, we (the international communist movement and the international proletariat) are not able to prevent world war through revolution and there is massive nuclear destruction, there will still be — and in some ways in concentrated form — the question of the future of humanity. This will then be a question acutely posed for resolution and will be resolved through armed conflict between forces representing diametrically and antagonistically opposed directions: back to the old relations, institutions, values, and ideologies to "reconstitute and rebuild" — *back to the same thing that led to this in the first place* — or on a radically new road, beginning on a primitive level but having learned more deeply and searingly where the old road leads, and embarking on a completely different course.

They are already preparing for this "aftermath" — yes, on top of all their plans that will lead to this devastation in the first place if they're not stopped! — and we must prepare for it too. But in fact our preparation is precisely the revolutionary work and revolutionary struggle being carried out by the international communist movement, waging revolutionary armed struggle where things are at that point and preparing for it where that is not yet the case. It is this that represents the real hope for humanity. Meeting the challenge to carry out and accelerate revolution and under all circumstances see the struggle through to the abolition of this monster, imperialism and all systems based on exploitation and enforced by murder and destruction — this is the meaning of taking responsibility for the future of humanity. It is a task that must be shouldered by the international proletariat and the international communist movement.

V.

Leadership . . .
and Other Philosophical Questions

Some Important Questions Concerning Leadership

The questions posed in relation to the novel *Water Margin* (in the broadest sense, as discussed in chapter two) find a concentrated expression, assume a concentrated form, with regard to leading people in the revolutionary movement. Indeed this was exactly what Mao had in mind in raising this in the first place. Among such leaders the question poses itself very sharply — and repeatedly, though in different forms — do you want to and do you strive to completely uproot the old order and remake the world entirely, from bottom to top, or just get your share of this rotting, dying old world (whose death, however, will not be gradual and painless but will come through acute and cataclysmic episodes)? This is a major dividing line between revolution and reform, even very militant reformism, and between Marxism and revisionism. To think that this question has ever been answered once and for all is already to begin to give the wrong answer: you have to "prove it all night," continuously and repeatedly — and particularly at each decisive stage.

Dare to Lead

At its meeting in 1979 the Central Committee of our party focused, among other important questions, on the challenges posed to leading people in confronting the task of carrying out a proletarian revolution in a country such as the U.S. with its powerful pulls toward capitulation and seeking the seemingly "comfortable" way out.[195] Clearly, these challenges too are magnified many times in a period such as this with the stakes as high and the possibilities — for historic advance or crushing defeat — as sharply in relief as they are. What this underlines is the crucial question of being prepared for sudden turns and leaps in the situation, dramatic and drastic changes, perhaps with little warning — all of which will also find concentrated expression in the approaching conjuncture. This is a question Lenin emphasized particularly in the context of World War 1, for example in *The Collapse of the Second International.*[196] And Mao even stated that "sudden changes are the most fundamental laws of the universe."[197] I don't believe this represents a different viewpoint than Mao's analysis that "the law of contradiction in things, that is, the law of the unity of opposites, is the basic law of materialist dialectics, . . . the fundamental law of nature and of society and therefore also the fundamental law of thought."[198] Rather, in calling sudden changes the basic law(s) of the universe, Mao is stressing a most important aspect of the law of contradiction: at a certain point in the struggle of opposites there is a *leap* which brings about a qualitative change in the thing (contradiction); and such changes are likely to — in a certain sense cannot help but — come suddenly, or they would not be leaps.

There is a dialectical relationship — there is unity as well as opposition — between authority, including the "cult of the personality (or personalities)" of leading people on the one hand and collectivity/collective leadership on the other hand. And in turn there is a dialectical relationship between this collective leadership and centralism on the one hand and diversity and initiative throughout the ranks of the party members on the other.

[195] "The Prospects for Revolution and the Urgent Tasks in the Decade Ahead," *Revolution*, Vol. 4, No. 10-11, pp. 7-9.

[196] See Lenin, *The Collapse of the Second International*, *LCW*, Vol. 21, pp. 207-59, especially p. 243.

[197] Mao, "Example of Dialectics," *Miscellany*, Part I, p. 219.

[198] Mao, *On Contradiction*, *MSW*, Vol. 1, pp. 311, 345.

(These same questions, which pose themselves within the party as the contradiction between leadership and membership, pose themselves more broadly in society as the contradiction between the party as a whole and the nonparty masses.)

As discussed — in hopefully a somewhat "trippy" way — earlier, in communist society there will still be the necessity for centralism and for leadership in a certain sense, but the ways must be found to prevent this from becoming the institutionalized authority or power of particular individuals or groups, installed as more or less permanent leaders. It should also be said that when communism has been reached there will not only be no need for such things as the cult of the personality but such things would be contrary to and harmful to the needs of society at that stage. This, however, is *not* true now. In this we can learn from Mao who pointed out:

> The question at issue is not whether or not there should be a cult of the individual, but rather whether or not the individual concerned represents the truth. If he does, then he should be revered. If truth is not present, even collective leadership will be no good. Throughout its history, our Party has stressed the combination of the role of the individual with collective leadership. . . . Some people opposed Lenin, saying that he was a dictator. Lenin's reply was straightforward: better that I should be a dictator than you![199]

The point is that in class society and with the division of labor (or significant remnants of the division of labor) characteristic of class-divided society, it is the case that certain individuals come to "represent the truth" in a concentrated way (as others do the false). This, of course, is not a "once-and-for-all, lifetime-guaranteed" thing — and there is always the danger that building up such people could turn into a very bad thing if they no longer did "represent the truth" after a certain point. But even

[199] Mao, "Talks at the Chengtu Conference (March 1958)," in Schram, ed., *Chairman Mao Talks to the People*, p. 100.

if there remains the real possibility that the individual may thus change, there will also remain the need for building up others who do continue to stand for the truth in a concentrated way. In any case such people play their role as leaders of a class (that is the meaning of Lenin's comment to those who called him a dictator — better me than you, better the proletariat than the bourgeoisie) and thus there is, as Mao described it, the combination of the role of the individual (in particular in this context the individual leader) and collective leadership.

Again, when humanity has advanced to communism, it will no longer be the case that particular individuals are more identified than others with "representing the truth" (this will be so around different specific questions but not in general). And thus "cults" of the individual will have no basis and could have no positive role, but would represent an impediment to the continuing development and transformation of the material world, of society and people, in accordance with the basic laws of the universe. Since, however, this is not the case now and "cults of the individual" can play a positive role (if and so long as "the individual concerned represents the truth"), then the task is to correctly handle the relations between this and collective leadership and more generally between collectivity and diversity, between centralism and individual initiative.

However much it may drive liberals, social democrats, and bourgeois democrats generally up a wall, there is also a dialectical relation — unity as well as opposition — between cult(s) of the individual around leading people and on the other hand ease of mind and liveliness, initiative, and creative, critical thinking among party members and the masses following the party. In the future communist society, this need for firmly established revolutionary authority as an "anchor" will no longer exist and would run counter to developing the critical spirit and critical thinking; it too will have to be abolished as an important part of the advance to communism. But to demand its abolition now runs counter to that advance, and to unleashing and developing that critical spirit and critical thinking.

A COMMUNIST VIEW OF COMMUNISM

The Revolutionary Communist Versus the Soviet Revisionist View of the Forces Producing Change

Obviously this is a gigantic subject and here I will focus on summarizing a few basic points.

In *For a Harvest of Dragons*, in the course of making a more thorough examination of the basic outlook, method, and objectives of the Soviet revisionists in contrast to that of genuine Marxism (which today means Marxism-Leninism-Mao Tsetung Thought), I pointed to a fundamental difference: the Soviet revisionists and their theoreticians regard laws in nature and society as some kind of ideal and metaphysical categories — categories that are fixed, frozen, and absolute, and which transcend material reality while imposing themselves on it — but in fact, and in the understanding of revolutionary communists, laws are derived from and reflect material reality. They refer to the essence and identity of things, but

> these things are in contradiction, in motion, and in the process of change, both within themselves and in interaction with other things. Thus laws, while they do profoundly reflect material reality, are not frozen or absolute.[200]

What are the larger social and political implications of this, of these fundamentally opposed viewpoints and methods?

Is the proletarian revolution with its goal of communism to be seen as the product and outcome of a straight-line march through history, on an essentially predetermined course? Or is it the result of spiral-like motion through contradiction, not

[200] Avakian, *For a Harvest of Dragons*, p. 131.

everywhere taking the same, more or less laid-out path, through all the same exact stages, but *having* led (as opposed to "bound to lead" or even "leading") to imperialism as a world system whose contradictions pose the necessity for proletarian revolution throughout the world as the only resolution that can lead society forward — that can liberate the forces of production, including most significantly the people? Our revolutionary communist outlook, which gives the latter answer, also shows that communism is not the *inevitable* resolution of these contradictions, in the sense of being the only possible one. The comment in the *Communist Manifesto* that class struggles throughout history have "each time ended, either in a revolutionary reconstitution of society at large, *or in the common ruin of the contending classes*"[201] has some relevance in relation to the question of world war and nuclear devastation. But, as stressed many times, even this would not eliminate the class struggle, including intense class struggle in the aftermath of this war and devastation (unless it did eliminate humanity). Exactly because this would be a question of struggle, however, its outcome cannot be predetermined; nor is it inconceivable that nuclear destruction would be so complete that human civilization would essentially (or even perhaps literally) die out. For these reasons it cannot be correctly said that communism is the inevitable resolution of the contradictions of imperialism. But this is no reason to become politically paralyzed; rather it is all the more reason to urgently intensify our work to accelerate the process of revolution in the U.S. and worldwide.

In all cases, it remains true that only with the achievement of communism — a society, a world, without classes, commodity production, and other property relations of exploitation and oppression, and the politics and ideology corresponding to this — only then will such things as war, poverty amidst mighty productive forces, national and sexual oppression, and the thousand other evils of life under the present order be abolished. The

[201] Marx and Engels, *Communist Manifesto*, p. 33, emphasis added.

proletariat with its communist vanguard is the driving force of the advance to communism because communism does correspond to the fundamental interests of the proletariat, and of no other class, and because the proletariat, and proletariat alone, is capable of carrying this process through. It is in the light of all this that the correct meaning and importance of the historic mission of the proletariat in bringing about communism can and must be understood.

Further on — and Away from — the Negation of the Negation

In *Mao Tsetung's Immortal Contributions*, in summarizing Mao's criticism of the concept of the negation of the negation — and his insistence that this is not a basic law of dialectics, which it had been classically held to be by Marxists — I pointed to the application of this "specifically in regard to the development of society," where

> the concept of the negation of the negation will tend to present a "closed system" of development leading to communism and promote a static, "absolutist" view of communism itself as the end product of the negation of the negation and the kingdom of "great harmony." As opposed to this, Mao declares in his 1964 talk on philosophy: "Communism will last for thousands and thousands of years. I don't believe that there will be no qualitative changes under communism, that it will not be divided into stages by qualitative changes! I don't believe it! . . . This is unthinkable in the light of dialectics."[202]

Here, in concluding this book, it seems appropriate to focus

[202] Avakian, *Mao Tsetung's Immortal Contributions*, p. 185; for Mao Tsetung's remarks see also "Talk on Questions of Philosophy (August 18, 1964)," in Schram, ed., *Chairman Mao Talks to the People*, p. 227. For further critical comments on the question of the "negation of the negation," see Bob Avakian, "More on the Question of Dialectics," *RW*, No. 95 (March 6, 1981), p. 3.

on another important aspect of this, as applied to the historical development of human society and its implications in the immediate situation before us:

It is not correct to picture "primitive communism" (the stage of society before classes emerged) as "pure" or without any seeds of oppression and to view the communist future as a return on a higher level to that pristine state. Nor is it necessary, or helpful, to depict things in these terms in order to be convinced of the possibility of achieving communism and to win others to fight for this and the radical rupture it will mean in relation to all previous society. There is plenty of basis at this stage of history and in today's world to achieve communism *and* to see the urgent necessity of fighting to achieve it — though that fight will be long, arduous, and tortuous — by straining to make the key breakthroughs and leaps toward that communist future that are demanded now.